THE
TREASURE OF
SUTTON HOO

BOOKS BY

Bernice Grohskopf

THE TREASURE OF SUTTON HOO:
SHIP-BURIAL FOR AN ANGLO-SAXON KING   1970

FROM AGE TO AGE: LIFE AND LITERATURE
IN ANGLO-SAXON ENGLAND   1968

SEEDS OF TIME: SELECTIONS FROM SHAKESPEARE   1963

THE
TREASURE OF
SUTTON HOO

*Ship-Burial for
an Anglo-Saxon King*

BERNICE GROHSKOPF

Atheneum   NEW YORK

1973

To Charles W. Phillips

Quotations from *Beowulf* are taken from *Beowulf*, translated by Burton Raffel. Copyright © 1963 by Burton Raffel. Reprinted by arrangement with The New American Library, Inc., New York.

Preface to the Paperback Edition

THIRTY-FOUR YEARS have passed since the excavation of the Sutton Hoo ship-burial in Suffolk, England, yet careful study of the treasure continues. My interest in the Sutton Hoo excavation began while I was at work on an introductory book on early English literature, and at first curiosity, then enthusiasm, led me to learn all I could of this true buried-treasure tale so that I might bring the story to American readers.

Since publication of the first edition of this book in 1970, further analysis of the objects in the British Museum laboratory along with comparison with available documents and other archaeological finds from the Anglo-Saxon period have resulted in new, although not necessarily conclusive, findings. One important revision, that of the stringed musical instrument, was released just before the 1970 publication of this book, and I discussed that alteration in the Appendix.

There have been other new findings: After long and painstaking study, the helmet, one of the most important objects, has been reconstructed. There were not only decorative changes—a third dragon head at the back of the crest, and rearrangement of the other two heads—but alterations in construction show it to have been a more practical, comfortable, close-fitting headpiece, with smaller eye openings and a longer neck guard, thus providing more protection for the wearer. The helmet is of special interest because it is Swedish, not Anglo-Saxon, and this rare find confirms theories of close ties with

Scandinavia long before the Viking Age, and, possibly, of a Swedish origin for the East Anglian royal house (see page 130).

Continued study of the hoard of gold coins, the major clue to dating the burial, favors the date of c. 625–630 for the gathering of the thirty-seven coins. It has been suggested that the weight of the coins, plus the blanks and ingots, represented the wergild, or blood-price, of a free man, according to Kentish laws of that time. It has also been speculated that the forty gold pieces, (thirty-seven coins plus three blanks) might have been payment for the forty oarsmen who were supposed to row the ship to its destination. Confirmation of the early date for the coins leads many scholars to favor the theory that the burial was a memorial for Redwald.

The bronze stag (photo page 78) was formerly believed to belong atop the standard, but further study showed it to have been the missing piece from the top of the whetstone, or stone sceptre (page 80–81). The stag, mounted on an iron-wire ring, which in turn was on a bronze pedestal, fitted one end of the stone sceptre perfectly. The other end of the sceptre, with its shallow bronze saucer, might fit the knee when held by a seated person. Thus, held upright with stag and ring at the top, it might have served as a royal ceremonial piece. It is interesting that the bronze stag was at first believed to belong to the helmet, then to the standard, also an emblem of royal office. Since there was no evidence of a missing piece from the standard, while there was such evidence on the sceptre, the stag was finally found to fit it. But the full meaning of the sceptre and the significance of the bronze saucer or the red-painted knobs and the eight carved faces have not been established. There

iv

is little doubt that it was a pagan ceremonial piece that was considered to have some magic power.

Further analysis of the shield-remains revealed the decorative bird figure to be more hawklike, with forked tail, greatly similar to bird brooches from the Uppland district of late fifth- and early sixth-century Sweden. The small dragon heads around the shield rim had probably been grouped in pairs. The detached "sword ring," a sign of nobility, that had been found in the area of the shield might belong to it, not to the sword. Shields with similar features have been found in boat-graves in the Swedish cemetery at Vendel, although not so elaborate as the Sutton Hoo shield.

The former restoration of the drinking horns was incorrect and a new construction revealed that in place of one enormous drinking horn there were two horns of smaller mouth-diameter, but of the same length, no doubt a pair from the same aurochs. The six smaller vessels were not horns, but round maplewood bottles whose cylindrical necks were decorated with ornamental, silver-gilt panels. They were probably a set.

Many of the questions about the Sutton Hoo ship-burial that were discussed in Chapter Three remain unanswered. All the more reason for one to ask why no progress has been made toward further excavations at Sutton Hoo. Eleven mounds remain unopened, two of which, according to R. L. S. Bruce-Mitford, Keeper of Medieval and Later Antiquities in the British Museum, are very likely undisturbed boat-burials.

I make no pretense of being a professional archaeologist or art historian, and for those readers who are interested in detailed analysis of the objects I recommend Dr. Bruce-Mitford's *Handbook*, published by the British

Museum, and his forthcoming four-volume study of the finds, the first volume of which was due in June 1973.

I want to thank Dr. Bruce-Mitford for having sent information and photos on some of the latest findings. Above all, I am indebted, once again, to Charles W. Phillips, the director of the 1939 excavation, for having kept me continually informed on all the latest developments regarding Sutton Hoo.

Although study of the finds continues, the story of the excavation remains, still, an exciting tale of one of the richest treasures ever dug in England and the most important archaeological document yet found from the Anglo-Saxon period.

August, 1973

Preface

BY DR. RUPERT BRUCE-MITFORD

I DID NOT PLAY any part in the 1939 discovery of
the Sutton Hoo ship-burial, nor did I see the excavations. I remember attending, in uniform, in the
early months of the war, Mr. Charles Phillips' first
public account of his sensational discoveries, at the
Society of Antiquaries Rooms in Piccadilly. The
objects he found, with boxes full of fragmentary
matter from the burial, spent the war years down a
disused length of the London Underground Rail-
way, with the Elgin marbles and much else. Work
began on the elucidation of the finds in 1945, when
they could be unpacked again in the Museum. This
was the phase when the British Museum's Research
Laboratory made its basic contribution. It was not
until 1946 that I had anything to do with Sutton
Hoo. Since then, however, my connection with the
find has been continuous. But from time to time others have been just as intimately associated with the
material, indeed more so. Making initial sense of the
fragments of drinking horns, helmet, and shield, for

instance, and the re-creating of these objects as we
have since known them, was mostly the work of the
brain and hands of Mr. Herbert Maryon. Maryon
was then already elderly, a retired Professor of
Sculpture and a metallurgist, especially interested in
the technology of early antiquities and works of art.
The Trustees of the British Museum recruited him
for the difficult task of reconstructing the more
complex pieces. His enthusiasm, persistence, skill,
and ingenuity were admirable, and publicly recognized. However, it is a fact that in the fifteen years
since Maryon's time conservation techniques and
scientific possibilities have advanced dramatically.
The British Museum, with its eminent Research
Laboratory, always a leader in this field, has taken
full advantage of these developments. Younger
helpers are playing a notable part in the current
work. I believe that it will be recognized that the
lapse of time between the plentiful early publications of the find, and the definitive account, though
regretted, has been vital. Had the finds been ex-
haustively described early on, they would, in the
majority of cases, have been described wrongly.
The definitive account which the Museum now has
in hand will have a substance and validity which
could not have been achieved twenty, fifteen, or
even ten years ago.

It is also possible, with this lapse of time and with new knowledge, to assess the discovery better. As with all great discoveries, the reality exceeds the first enthusiastic cries. The ship-burial was not a seven-day wonder. It is a new rung established in the ladder of history, and throws a great deal of light on the period of Anglo-Saxon origins and consolidation.

Mrs. Grohskopf's initiative in wishing to bring knowledge of Sutton Hoo to a wider public, particularly to the American public, is timely. For Sutton Hoo has a future which will soon begin to unfold. There is the rest of the site to excavate. Though the chances of finding another undisturbed grave, let alone one approaching the ship-burial in richness, are remote, important information is bound to emerge. And the definitive publication will call for assimilation and comment when it appears. But apart from being timely, Mrs. Grohskopf's work will have a deeper value. Even at a distance of a millenium and more it is salutary for us to know the background from which so much that we have inherited has sprung. We become aware of a continuing human dignity, and realize that love of beauty, joy in creation, perfection in craftsmanship, are basic instincts in man, manifest even in the black days when the civilization of

Rome had been overwhelmed and the Barbarians were slowly laying the foundations of the medieval and modern world amidst the ruins.

Mrs. Grohskopf has skilfully placed this great archaeological discovery, sympathetically described, in its contemporary setting, painting in the background and giving it context. I welcome her book warmly and wish it every success.

The British Museum
July 1969

Foreword

BY C. W. PHILLIPS

THE EXCAVATION OF the Sutton Hoo ship-burial in 1939 was, as far as Great Britain was concerned, one of the principal liberating forces in the field of archaeology for a century. It had the effect of an explosion, but world events were to muffle its full effect for seven years; it is a tribute to its power that the finds continue to provoke a steady stream of study and comment thirty years after the event. The dig was almost a chance happening, and the sudden confrontation of the state archaeological service with this unexpected challenge against a background of growing emergency and alarm led to a series of improvisations which placed the events at Sutton Hoo in 1939 squarely into the hands of a mainly amateur team which had to sink or swim as best it could. This was quite in the British tradition. There was no time to seek the advice of Continental colleagues experienced with this type of site, and the whole piece had to be played by ear. The imposed time limit may have been a positive advantage. While undue haste leading to carelessness may be disastrous to an excavation, the spectacle of the long-protracted and desperately cautious proceedings in some modern excavations is not reassuring, especially in the light of today's costs. Provided the work is done with care and due thought, the addition of the factor speed is a great gain. Sutton Hoo was carried through at a public charge of less than £100, and in view of the subsequent great generosity of Mrs. Pretty, the legal owner of the treasure, in presenting the finds to the nation, it was the best single investment our rulers have ever made in the field of archaeology.

The immediate effect of the Sutton Hoo find has been to stimulate further work in all branches of Anglo-Saxon archaeology. The find has peculiar interest because it occupies a midway position when paganism was not yet extinct, but was being rapidly supplanted by Christianity. Nothing had been found before 1939 that gave any real idea of the rich background of Anglo-Saxon kingship, the technical resources which could be deployed by the more important kingdoms of the Heptarchy, and their far-ranging foreign contacts. Something of this might have been suspected from great engineering works like the Wansdyke, the Cambridgeshire Dykes, and Offa's Dyke dividing the Mercians from the Welsh. All of these involved great exercises of power, but otherwise, with the exception of a fair number of richly furnished graves, much of the surviving evidence of early Anglo-Saxon life was pitched at the low level of miserable huts and a humble peasant existence. It is true that the evidence of a historian like Bede suggests better things, and Anglo-Saxon poems like *Beowulf* depict a heroic society rich in gold and possessions, but there was no solid reason for regarding these as unaffected by poetic license. Sutton Hoo has come as a startling confirmation that they told no more than the truth.

Since 1946 a number of excavations have revealed the halls of King Edwin of Northumbria at Yeavering; a royal residence of the Kings of Wessex at Cheddar; the high achievement of early monastic houses like Jarrow and Wearmouth; and the capital of the later Anglo-Saxon kings of England at Winchester. This activity has also spread out into the Celtic world at Tintagel, Glastonbury, Dinas Powys, Dinorben, Dinas Emrys, and complex Scottish sites like Jarlshof in Shetland. Reaching back towards Roman times, some light at least is being thrown on the misty age of Arthur and the hitherto unsuspected contacts of the Celtic world with the Mediterranean. The military works of Alfred and his successors built against the invading Danes are being recognized and studied, while towns like Southampton, Stamford, Ipswich, and Thetford are now illustrating the growth of urban life and trading contacts. A new age has also dawned in the study of Anglo-Saxon coinage. Some of this is due to opportunities given by the destructions of war, but the stimulus of Sutton Hoo is undeniable.

Last, the boundary of the Norman Conquest has been transcended, and there has been a notable revival of medieval field archaeology seeking the origins of the medieval castle, establishing effective pottery sequences, probing the secrets of the early manor house and the sites of long-deserted villages, and generally breaking out of the shackles which tended to limit practical interest in this field until quite recently. The whole study of the migration and medieval periods has made a great leap forward.

It only remains for me to commend Mrs. Grohskopf's account of the Sutton Hoo dig to American readers, and hope that it may stimulate further interest in the origins which many of us share in common.

Acknowledgments

I WANT TO THANK Dr. R. L. S. Bruce-Mitford, Keeper of Medieval and Later Antiquities at the British Museum, for his generous cooperation, and for his offer to read the typescript of this book for factual errors. His invaluable *Handbook* was always on my desk as I wrote, and I trust that I have acknowledged my debt to him by putting together a book that reflects, even in a small way, his high standards of careful and thorough scholarship.

Members of Dr. Bruce-Mitford's staff have also been helpful: Miss Angela Evans, Miss Joyce Davis, and Mrs. Leslie Webster. I am grateful to the British Museum for granting permission to use the photographs.

Professor W. F. Grimes, Director of the Institute of Archaeology at London University, generously took an hour from a busy schedule to talk with me about his part in the excavation. Mrs. M. C. Barton, the present owner of Sutton Hoo Estates, was kind enough to permit me on her property to see the ship-grave. Mr. Paul Johnstone, Senior Producer, Archaeology and History Unit, of the BBC, arranged to have the film "Million Pound Grave" shown to me privately. It is an excellent photographic record of the dig including interviews with all who were involved with the ship-burial excavation. Mr. Johnstone's assistant, Miss Arline Firth, extended herself most cordially, and I am grateful for her help. I also want to thank Mr. Colin L. Robertson, Librarian at the British Information Services, who went out of his way to answer questions.

It was my husband who encouraged me to make the trip to England so that I could do research on Sutton Hoo, and from the beginning of the book right through the final draft, his continuing enthusiasm, suggestions, and criticisms have been invaluable to me.

Above all, I am indebted to Mr. Charles W. Phillips, who conducted the ship-burial excavation at Sutton Hoo, for his generous cooperation on this book. I shall long treasure the memory of the day I spent talking with Mr. Phillips at his home in Surrey. The story of the Sutton Hoo ship-burial is Mr. Phillips' story, and it is with gratitude and respect that I dedicate this book to him.

Contents

xvii

CONTENTS

Illustrations

CHAPTER ONE

THE DIG

*Take these treasures, earth, now that no one
Living can enjoy them. They were yours, in the
    beginning;
Allow them to return. War and terror
Have swept away my people, shut
Their eyes to delight and to living, closed
The door to all gladness. No one is left
To lift these swords, polish these jeweled
Cups: no one leads, no one follows. These ham-
    mered
Helmets, worked with gold, will tarnish
And crack; the hands that should clean and polish
    them
Are still forever. And these mail shirts, worn
In battle, once, while swords crashed
And blades bit into shields and men,
Will rust away like the warriors who owned them.
None of these treasures will travel to distant
Lands, following their lords. The harp's
Bright song, the hawk crossing through the hall
On its swift wings, the stallion tramping
In the courtyard—all gone, creatures of every
Kind, and their masters, hurled to the grave!*

BEOWULF: 2247–2266

Preliminary Excavations at Sutton Hoo

O N JULY 26, 1939, the London *Times* ran the following news item:

GRAVE OF AN ANGLO-SAXON CHIEF

It was learned yesterday that the burial place of an early Anglo-Saxon Chief, dating in all probability from the sixth century, had been unearthed in Suffolk. The body of the dead chief had been laid in a large rowing boat, which had been drawn up from the water and placed bodily in a deep grave. The grave dug for the reception of the boat had a length of 82 feet and a beam of 16 feet. Nothing remains of it but a pattern of iron clench nails in the ground, but finds of considerable antiquarian interest accompanied the body. These have been removed by excavators on behalf of the

3

Ancient Monuments Department of the Office of Works.

This was the first public announcement of the most remarkable archaeological find in England's history, and it was tucked away on the entertainment page under a notice of George Bernard Shaw's eighty-third birthday. The news had leaked out before the archaeologists were ready to make it public, and the brief report was incorrect, in part. The value of the treasure, untouched for nearly thirteen centuries, was estimated at more than a million dollars, but the historical value is inestimable.

For the first time scholars would be able to examine the actual regalia of a king who reigned in England during the Anglo-Saxon period. This period extended from the mid-fifth century to 1066, when the Normans came and conquered the Germanic inhabitants of England. English history since the Norman Conquest is well documented, but the history of the Anglo-Saxon period has been pieced together from historical, literary, and archaeological documents. Its first hundred and fifty years are shrouded in mystery; no written records, no monuments, no ruins of cities remain. Scholars have studied histories written during that time in other lands, and they have studied the fragmentary evidence turned up by archaeologists. But Anglo-Saxon archaeology is a comparatively recent study. For many years finds from the Anglo-Saxon period were incorrectly identified as Roman. Of the 25,000 pagan graves dating from the period, no grave, even the richest,* has ever yielded such a wealth of treasure and information as that at Sutton Hoo.

The story of the treasure at Sutton Hoo began in the summer of 1938 when Mrs. E. M. Pretty, the owner of a property called Sutton Hoo, decided to have a group of eleven earth mounds ** on her land investigated. Barrows are not uncommon in Suffolk, and like other mounds in the area, they had long been assumed to date from the Bronze Age, about 1500 B.C. But Mrs. Pretty was curious, perhaps because of an old story told in the nearby town of Woodbridge, that back in 1810 a ploughman had found a lovely circular brooch on the land. Rumors of buried treasure persisted, but no one had investigated until Mrs. Pretty became the owner of the land.

---

* The grave of a chieftain dating from the early seventh century was found at Taplow, Buckinghamshire in 1883. The chieftain had been buried in gold-embroidered robes, and the grave contained a few fine pieces of jewellery.
** Subsequently, five more mounds were recognized.

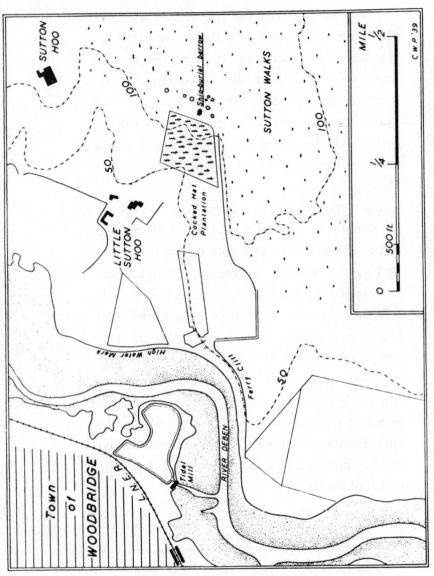

Map of a-town of Woodbridge showing the location of Sutton Hoo and the ship burial barrow

CWP '39

1: The Dig

At her request the authorities at nearby Ipswich Museum agreed to begin excavating and assigned Mr. Basil Brown to the job. He was offered a room at Mrs. Pretty's home, a salary of thirty-five shillings a week, and a staff consisting of two of Mrs. Pretty's estate gardeners, Mr. Jacobs and Mr. Spooner. Mr. Brown did not have great expectations. Nearly all of the mounds appeared to have been disturbed by robbers, and he had little hope of finding anything of value. It is to Mr. Brown's credit that, despite his realistic outlook, he went about his task with great care. During 1938 three of the mounds were excavated by Mr. Brown and his crew with comparatively unexciting results. First of all, they found that earlier excavations had been done by rabbits. As they expected, they also found that treasure hunters had carried off all but a few objects. But what they did find was of significant interest.

Mound No. 3, the first to be excavated, had not been robbed, and the contents of the grave indicated that a person of high rank had been cremated there. They found an engraved limestone plaque unlike anything known from the period, as well as a unique bronze lid, an iron axe head, pottery sherds, bits of textile, remains of a blue glass bowl, and fragments of cremated bone, all of which lay on a concave wooden tray, about six feet long, much decomposed.

The next to be opened, Mound No. 2, was the second largest of the group, about 100 feet across and nearly 8 feet high. When opening such mounds the archaeologist does not simply grab a shovel and heave to. He first studies the best way to lay out an approach trench so that digging can proceed with the least possible damage to the objects buried there. At the start of digging Mound No. 2, Mr. Brown came upon objects of great interest, the finding of which would soon prove invaluable: two small iron clumps, much corroded, but closely resembling the iron clench nails that had been found at an excavation in 1862 of an Anglo-Saxon boat. This, the Snape boat-grave, only nine miles from Sutton Hoo, was the first Anglo-Saxon boat-burial found.* Mr. Brown had come upon another boat-grave.

As they continued digging, they found unmistakable evidence that the grave had been robbed. Ar-

* Techniques of excavation and of recording were primitive at that time, and of the few things found in the grave, some have disappeared. One beautiful and extremely rare gold ring with a black onyx intaglio disappeared for years and finally turned up, having been in the possession of one of the excavators who simply chose to keep it as a memento, and pass it on to his heirs. His son, having realized its historical importance, fortunately willed it to the British Museum. Other finds from the Snape boat-grave are at the Ipswich Museum.

chaeologists can tell by examining the soil when a
pit has been dug and then filled in. As they removed the "fill" from the pit, the distinct outline of
a boat left by the decayed timber was revealed in
the sand. The boat had been about 18 feet long,
smaller than the Snape boat. What little remained
of the treasure that robbers had not carried away
gave ample indication that, like the previous
mound, it had been a rich grave. Fragments of
ornamental gilt bronze and silver gilt foil, a silver
buckle-loop, a bronze ring, the tip of a sword found
pointing upward, and other grave furnishings indicated that the robbers, whoever and whenever they
were, had carried off a rich store of treasure.

Mound No. 4 had been so thoroughly looted that
only fragments of bronze, a part of what may have
been an ivory gaming piece, and calcined bone remained. Historians have studied the findings in
these graves, along with Mr. Brown's notes and
diagrams, in minute detail.*

The results of the 1938 excavations at Sutton
Hoo proved to be no more exciting than previous
Anglo-Saxon excavations. But Mr. Brown thought
it worth while to continue, and Mrs. Pretty agreed.

* An account by Dr. R. L. S. Bruce-Mitford of the 1938 findings appeared in the *Proceedings of the Suffolk Institute of
Archaeology*, Vol. XXX, Part I, 1965, with photos of the objects.

On May 8, 1939, Mrs. Pretty and Mr. Brown were surveying the mounds, discussing how to proceed, when Mrs. Pretty pointed to the largest of the mounds and asked, "What about this one?" *
With that off-hand direction, Mr. Brown began the dig that would prove to be England's most exciting archaeological find.

Finding the Ship-Burial

Mound No. 1 was the largest of the barrows, roughly 100 feet long by 75 feet wide and 9 feet high. Earth had been removed from the western end some time ago, making it difficult to guess precisely how large it had been. The entire area of the Sutton Hoo mounds was a typical sandy heath with a thick layer of bracken; the mounds of various sizes occurred at intervals and appeared at first glance to be merely accidental rises in the land.

Mr. Brown began digging the largest mound from the east end, driving a trench right through the middle, as though he were cutting a huge center slice from a cake. The work had not progressed very far when one of the gardeners came upon

* Charles Green, *Sutton Hoo*, Merlin Press, London, 1963, p. 29.

several clumps of corroded iron embedded in the sand, and removing one, called Mr. Brown, who immediately recognized them as clench nails in position. Had he not had the experience of finding and identifying clench nails during the earlier excavations, Mr. Brown very likely would not so quickly have identified this as another ship-burial. He could not, however, at this early stage, anticipate the size of the ship.

As they continued clearing from one end, Mr. Brown was careful to see that the nails, which now began to appear in a regular pattern, remained in position. As the earth was removed, bit by bit, the forward part of the ship emerged in rough outline until, moving toward the center, they cleared to the eleventh frame, or rib, and reached what they believed was a burial chamber. When fragments of iron, wood, and bronze came into view, Mr. Brown realized he had come upon something of enormous importance.

Just as they had anticipated, the archaeologists found evidence that treasure hunters had got there first. The robbers had dug quite deeply into what they calculated was the exact center of the mound, where they were certain to find something. But when they reached what they recognized to be the original ground surface under the mound without finding any treasure, the robbers stopped digging. From the evidence found by the excavators, the robbers, having grown weary and hungry, built a fire to cook a meal, and had a drink from a tiger-ware jug that they tossed away and broke. Then they packed up and left, never knowing that ten feet below them lay the treasure of Sutton Hoo.

Archaeology is a comparatively new science, for many years having been mere treasure hunting for the sake of the monetary value, not the historical value, of any finds. Robbers plundered old graves, carried off valuables, and, in their hurry and igno-rance, destroyed the everyday objects that might have thrown light on our knowledge and under-standing of former cultures. Much has been de-stroyed through carelessness, ploughed under by farmers, or buried forever when buildings were constructed for a growing industrial population. Regrettably, archaeologists of the nineteenth cen-tury, in their enthusiasm, blundered with improper tools, often causing the already disintegrating relics to crumble completely.

From a study of the tigerware jug, the excavators were able to date the robbery to the late sixteenth or early seventeenth century. The robbers had missed the treasure simply because the conforma-tion of the mound, somewhat altered at one end by ploughing, led them to miscalculate the center, leaving the burial chamber and the treasure untouched for another 240 years.

The second week in June the burial chamber was reached, and word had begun to leak out that an unusual archaeological dig was going on at Sutton Hoo. Mr. C. W. Phillips, Fellow of the Society of Antiquaries, and a graduate of Cambridge University, happened to be in the area on business, and quite by chance, the gentleman he was visiting mentioned the unusual dig, at that time rumored to be a Viking ship-burial of the ninth or tenth century. Mr. Phillips decided to go up to Sutton Hoo and see for himself. He described his remarkable experience: "When I crossed the short stretch of heath from Mrs. Pretty's house and saw the large dump of sand that had already been moved out of the excavation I had no clear idea of what I was going to see in a few moments. When it came the sight was a shock." * Enough earth had been removed to enable him to determine the unusual size of the ship, and from the conformation of the earth, the large burial chamber was apparent, with some of the contents faintly visible. Cauldrons, large

* C. W. Phillips, "The Excavation of the Sutton Hoo Ship-Burial," in *Recent Archaeological Excavations in Britain,* edited by R. L. S. Bruce-Mitford, Routledge and Kegan Paul, Ltd., London, 1956.

wooden pegs, and chain work were exposed. It must have been difficult to resist the temptation to dig in immediately and discover what else lay beneath the mound, but the material had to be covered and work halted until the archaeologists could proceed in an orderly way.

The first step was to have the dig declared an ancient monument and thus give it legal protection. The British Museum and the Office of Works were informed, and by the 10th of July, Mr. Phillips, at the request of the Office of Works, returned to supervise the excavation.

The summer of 1939 was an uneasy time. Europe was threatened by war, and few believed that England could stay out of it. Mr. Phillips realized that the excavation had to move ahead swiftly. With limited help and equipment, he set to work to find out about a period in the beginning of England's history when wars and threats of invasions had been as much a part of life as they were at that very moment.

Mr. Brown agreed to stay on to assist Mr. Phillips; Mrs. Pretty's gardeners continued to help. The area of the Sutton mounds is treeless, and for shelter the workers had a tiny shepherd's hut that they kept under a large shade tree in a nearby woods.

1: The Dig

Some of the workers began removing earth that had slid into the collapsed burial chamber, while others started to clear earth from the stern. The outline of the huge ship was perfect. Every vestige of wood had rotted, but what remained was a perfect impression of the ship's hull, which had been in the sand for centuries. The earth was stained from the wood, and the rusted iron clench nails that had once held the ship together remained exactly in place.

Sutton Hoo is on a steep slope about 100 feet above the River Deben, overlooking the inlet where the river flows into the North Sea. The mounds are half a mile inland, so that having been maneuvered up the embankment, the ship would have had to be hauled overland. Later in the course of the excavation, after a study of the ship mold, they determined that it had been made of oak, clinker-built, and had been about 89 feet long by 14 feet wide. They also learned that the ship had not been slid into the grave, but had been lowered, a process that must have required ingenuity and enormous manpower. Although no internal fittings of the ship remained, the archaeologists could tell that it had been rowed by 38 oarsmen, with a steersman at the helm.

It was immediately apparent that it was not a

View of the excavated ship, with work in progress.
The burial chamber has been cleared.

Viking ship, but was more primitive in construction. The excavators' excitement rose as their suspicions were confirmed that the ship dated from early Anglo-Saxon times. It was perhaps two hundred years older than any Viking ship-burial. In such a ship the Germanic invaders had come from their homes on the continent to invade Britain.

A Glimpse of England in the Seventh Century *

In the middle of the fifth century, after the Romans had left Britain, the island was invaded by Germanic tribes coming from coastal lands on the North Sea. The Saxons came from what we now call Holstein; the Angles occupied what is now Schleswig; the Jutes came from the mainland province of Denmark. Another tribe, the Frisians, occupied what is now Holland, from the Ems to the Rhine. The year when the invasions began cannot be pinpointed; some came while the Romans were still there, others later. But 449, the year given by Bede, the most reliable historian of the period, is near enough. The Saxons came not as invaders at

* Since written documentation of pagan and early Anglo-Saxon England is slight, many of the statements in this section are the result of calculated speculation.

first, but as hired mercenaries, summoned by a king named Vortigern to help him fight the Picts. They came in large enough numbers to settle, the Saxons in the south, the Angles in the north. They drove back the Celts, who, after four hundred years of Roman domination, had had only the briefest period of freedom from a conqueror's domination. Eventually, the distinction between Saxon and Angle was forgotten and the word *Saxones* applied to all the people. After a while the terms *Angli* and *Anglia* came to be used along with *Saxones*, until gradually *Angli* and *Anglia* took over completely. The earliest writings in the vernacular called the language *Englisc*, the people *Angelcynn*, or race of *Angles*. The word *Englaland*, land of the Angles, first appeared about 1000. The dialects of the invading tribes differed,* but their language, a Germanic one, was essentially the same, and from their language, their laws, their customs, the country we now call England developed.

Historians have comparatively few sources for the study of this early period in Anglo-Saxon history. With the exception of Bede's *Ecclesiastical*

---

* Most surviving manuscripts of the period are in the West Saxon dialect, the basis for our knowledge of Old English. Only the merest fragments written in the other dialects, Northumbrian, Mercian, and Kentish, remain. While they provide a basis for comparison, the material is too scant for linguists to make a thorough study.

1: The Dig

History of the English People completed in 731, the few histories written are not entirely reliable; charters and laws from a later time provide some information, but it is unwise to base assumptions about the early period on later evidence. The small body of literature that remains was recorded in the tenth century, but together with archaeological finds and place names, they provide merely fragments with which to piece together a patchwork picture of life in early Anglo-Saxon England.

The Sutton Hoo treasure is the outstanding archaeological document we have of that period in English history. The intrinsic value of the splendid 1300-year-old hoard is minor compared with its historical value, for here is the actual regalia of an Anglo-Saxon king—his symbols of sovereignty. The imprint of the ship enabled scholars to model a ship very like those in which invaders came to England. Revealed also were heirlooms from Sweden and rare silver pieces imported from foreign lands.

At the time of the burial, the early seventh century, Christianity had just been introduced to England. In 597, Pope Gregory sent St. Augustine to convert the heathen English. Gradually the new faith was accepted, but the people did not immediately abandon their pagan beliefs, so that throughout the literature one finds a mingling of pagan and Christian tradition. The Sutton Hoo burial, which probably took place less than thirty years after Christianity was introduced in East Anglia, revealed the same puzzling combination.

At the time of the invasion, England was a land of dense forests and marshland with some cultivated areas. Roman roads made a crosspatch pattern throughout the land, although the remains of Roman civilization had already begun to decay. The invading tribes apparently had little use for the civilized Roman homes, and evidence of their ignorance was found when remains of a Roman villa were excavated showing that a fire had been built in the middle of the mosaic tile floor. It is unlikely that the invaders' attacks were systematic and planned, although they were doubtless bloody. The invaders advanced through the country by road and river, settling in different places and forming small kingdoms, with several smaller satellites, more or less under one *Bretwalda*, or ruler of Britain. It did not mean that there was unity, or that there were no other kings, but one, more powerful than the others was the acknowledged leader to whom respect was paid and under whose leadership they fought. The title Bretwalda carried considerable prestige, but no formal rights were attendant on the title, and it shifted from one kingdom to another.

THE KING, THE PEOPLE, AND THE GOVERNMENT
During the Anglo-Saxon period, about 700 years, there were approximately 200 kings, some of whose names we do not even know. The word "king" is from the Old English *cyning*, his territory was his *cynedom*. How did a king become a king in Anglo-Saxon times? Royal genealogies exist, but they must be examined with care. Of the eight that survive from the seventh century, the ancestry of seven has been traced back to Woden, the chief pagan Teutonic god, so that one might easily doubt their reliability. Succession to the throne was not governed by primogeniture; no constitutional monarchy with defined rules of succession existed. A man could become king through inheritance, occasionally by election or designation. Sometimes a man became king simply because he had the greatest following and military strength. Any dispute over a claim to succession led to war, but the usurper, once he had proved his strength in battle, could support his shaky claim by declaring he had been designated, or "elected." In those days election did not mean what it does today; the Latin *eligere* and the Old English *ceosan* may have meant something

closer to the word "acknowledge" or "acclaim," for the people made no actual choice. Beowulf, for instance, succeeded to the throne of the Geats (southern Sweden) because he had been chosen by the former king's widow.

The ceremony in which a king in pagan times was formally declared a king is not known. Coronation as we know it today did not exist until the tenth century.* Germanic kings of the fifth and sixth centuries were confirmed by raising the king on a shield, but there is no record that this custom was followed in England. We know, from the Sutton Hoo grave, that symbols of sovereignty existed that no doubt were used for ceremonial occasions. Early tenth-century coins show King Athelstan (925–39) wearing a simple crown with unadorned prongs rising from the circlet.

The king was surrounded by loyal followers, the size of his following giving an indication of his power. It was a reciprocal relationship, the king providing a great hall, great feasts, and lavish rewards for courage and loyalty; the followers returning his generosity by surrendering their lives to his service. When not at war, the king and his companions spent their time riding, hunting, and

---

* Edgar was anointed and crowned in 973 at Bath by St. Dunstan of Canterbury in a ceremony that has been echoed down to the twentieth century.

attending to judicial matters. Since the king owned
the land, he was entitled to "food rent" from his
subjects. Since no stable currency existed, rent had
to be paid in wagon-loads of food. Each landowner
was obligated to supply sufficient food to the king
and his court for one day. This was called "farm of
one night." From the laws of King Ine of Wessex,
who died a century after the Sutton Hoo burial, we
have a list of the food rent from ten hides of land.
A hide of land varied from one locality to another,
but presumably it was the amount of land considered sufficient for one peasant household, *terra
unius familiae*. The size of a hide was determined
by the individual's living standards. Here is the list
of food rent from ten hides:

> Ten vats of honey, three hundred loaves,
> twelve "ambers" * of British ale, thirty "am-
> bers" of clear ale, two full-grown oxen or ten
> wethers, ten geese, twenty hens, ten cheeses,
> an "amber" full of butter, five salmon, twenty
> pounds' weight of fodder, and one hundred
> eels.**

The banquets at the great hall were well-sup-
plied, boisterous affairs. Everyone brought his own

* An Anglo-Saxon measure of dry or liquid quantity.
** F. M. Stenton, *Anglo-Saxon England*, Oxford University
Press, London, 1947, p. 285.

knife; there were no forks, and the beautiful glasses were tumblers with no base that had to be drained at one draught. One of the drinks was mead, thus the term mead-hall. The six-quart drinking horn found at Sutton Hoo gives evidence that drinking was indeed on a grand scale, and the horn, which cannot be put down when full, was passed around to the company until drained. The king, or lord, sat on a high seat in the center of the long side of the hall, with his queen, or lady, beside him. Songs were sung by scops to the accompaniment of a harp; stories of heroic exploits were told in song by the warriors, and as the evening wore on, the boasts of rewards received for service to their lords led to quarrels and, sometimes, serious fighting.

> The feast went on, laughter and music
> And the brave words of warriors celebrating
> Their delight.
>
> BEOWULF: 642–644

At some point in the evening, the lady would carry a jeweled goblet around for all to drink, and then, leaving the warriors to their carousing, depart for her separate chambers, where she was later joined by her lord.

Then Welthow went from warrior to warrior,
Pouring a portion from the jeweled cup

For each, till the bracelet-wearing queen
Had carried the mead-cup among them and it was
    Beowulf's
Turn to be served.

BEOWULF: 620–624

Comfort and privacy were luxuries only for nobility; the others slept in the hall on benches or on the floor, where mattresses and pillows had been strewn for the purpose. If there were windows, they had no glass, but since the only source of heat and light was the huge fireplace, the open window was a necessity. Sometimes there were only holes in the roof. The English climate at that time was no different from now, so the hall could not have been a cozy place for sleeping.

The relationship between the king and his followers, or *comitatus*,* was based on a bond of intense loyalty, and this theme recurs throughout the literature of the period. Loyalty to one's leader came above family loyalty. One fought for his king, lived for his king, died for his king. A warrior whose king was slain in battle died with him; vengeance was a duty. A warrior who returned

---

* *Gesith* was another term to describe a follower of the king. In the ninth century, thane was the term for a man in the king's service.

from battle leaderless was dishonored. The great man, the hero, was one whose physical courage and loyalty preserved the sanctity of the relationship to his lord. His tale was told in song and story over and over to an audience that never tired of hearing of manly valor in service to one's lord.

The power of the king was symbolized by his possessions, as well as by the size of his following, not unlike the present time when possessions signify status and income. The king's status symbols were his jewels, his personal regalia, the lavishness of his feasts, and the splendor of his hall and household possessions.

> he thought of greatness and resolved
> To build a hall that would hold his mighty
> Band and reach higher toward Heaven than
>   anything
> That had ever been known to the sons of men.
>
> BEOWULF: 67–70

From the descriptions in *Beowulf*, and from recent excavations at Yeavering in Northumberland,*

* After photographs taken from the air revealed the presence of postholes, excavations were carried out at Yeavering between 1953 and 1957 under the direction of B. K. Hope-Taylor. Photographs taken from the air when the sun is low reveal the difference in crop growth where land has been filled, changes that cannot be detected on the ground.

26

we have an idea of the dimensions and general layout of the royal residence. The Anglo-Saxons built with timber, and the shape of the king's hall was oblong, probably as long as 100 feet, with benches along the sides for sitting and sleeping. The floor was paved, perhaps quite decoratively, the fireplace was huge, and the main table at which the king sat was centrally placed. The hall was hung with splendid tapestry on special occasions; candles or braziers were used for light. The door was wide enough for men to enter on horses.

King Edwin, who reigned in Northumbria from 616 to 632, had his palace at Yeavering. Excavators found evidence of several large halls, two with porches at either end, surrounded by eleven somewhat smaller buildings, possibly the private halls of nobles in service to the king. Most interesting was a structure resembling a grandstand with a surprisingly large seating capacity, suggesting a meeting-place for law-making, or a moot. The excavators also found the remains of a church. Edwin had been a heathen who was converted by Paulinus, one of the missionaries sent by Pope Gregory in 601 to help Augustine. After he had been consecrated a bishop, Paulinus traveled to Northumbria with the Kentish princess who was to marry King Edwin of Northumbria. Eventually, Edwin accepted his bride's faith, but not before having called a meeting of his councillors to discuss the merits of the new religion. It is said that Paulinus preached at Yeavering for thirty-six days, converting those from surrounding villages who came to hear him.

The king's household traveled with him when he visited his royal estates and it must have required considerable preparation to entertain him. Fortunately, the king and his retinue did not "drop in" unexpectedly, but usually sent purveyors in advance to be certain there were adequate provisions. One of the public burdens borne by the peasant landholder was to offer hospitality to the king and his companions.

The king entertained visitors from surrounding areas as well as from foreign lands. His household was the government, and it consisted of his witan —the councillors or wise men—presumably chosen by the king. In pagan times the king's witan was made up of his thanes and ealdormen. In Christian times, bishops, archbishops, and abbots were part of the witan. The king's business was attended to by a representative, an ealdorman, appointed by the king, and in charge of at least one shire. Like the king, he could lead his forces in war and preside over any judicial assembly.

The structure of society in early Anglo-Saxon England, drawing on an early seventh-century manuscript, reveals that in Kent there were a class of nobles, or earls, and a class of independent peasant landholders, or ceorls, who were entitled to protection by law. Over-all assumptions, however, cannot be based on Kent's laws. Wergild, the economic value placed on a man's life, was the chief mark of distinction. It was the "man-price," the amount paid to a man's family or lord in case of his death or injury. The king's ealdorman had a wergild four times higher than the king's thane. That of the ceorl was lower, and varied from kingdom to kingdom.

Little is known of laws until the coming of Christianity, after which the church scribes recorded them. Judicial matters probably were handled by a public assembly of a shire presided over by the king's ealdorman. The term *folc moot* to refer to popular meetings was not used before Alfred's time. Kinship was a strong bond and a man's kinsmen were duty bound to help him when he was in trouble. A kinless man was indeed unfortunate.

TOWNS AND VILLAGES   Every village * had a public meeting-place, and we know that ceorls, or peasant landholders, lived in association with others, sharing

---

* There have been excavations in parts of England that will throw light on the layout of an Anglo-Saxon village, but nothing has as yet been published. In general, excavations are possible only when demolition is in progress, or after enemy action.

with neighboring ceorls the responsibility of supplying the king's food rent. This economic association was the true beginning of the English village. Taxation records appear in the eleventh century, indicating that England was divided into villages consisting of a certain number of hides. Probably these divisions occurred in the seventh century. There had to be some system of maintaining order, assessing taxes, and settling local disputes. Certain services were due the king besides offering hospitality and contributing food rent. Royal villages had to be built, bridges constructed, and strongholds fortified to defend the land. To administer these matters, there must have been a local assembly.

The Anglo-Saxon town was an economic center, a marketplace where people brought goods from surrounding farmlands, a place where they might buy glass or bronze, or other goods from abroad. Before coinage the exchange of goods was by barter.* Bede refers to London as a "metropolis" to which many came by land and sea. The findings at Sutton Hoo and at other Anglo-Saxon excavations reveal that there was, even in the early seventh cen-

* Anglo-Saxon gold coins were not struck until the middle or latter part of the seventh century, but foreign coins were evidently used. In the early eighth century, silver coins were minted in England.

30

tury, considerable trade with the continent. The Anglo-Saxons continued to use the roads built by the Romans, even though they did not know how to keep them in a state of repair. Manuscript drawings show two- and four-wheeled carts drawn either by men or by animals. Probably some goods were transported by water.

The cereals most commonly raised were barley, oats, and wheat; wool was the principal export. Those who were not noblemen in the king's service were shepherds, farmers, merchants, fishermen, hunters, shoemakers, and so forth. The art of the goldsmith was highly specialized, and he must have enjoyed a high social status, since he had ample time for his creative work. The Anglo-Saxons loved jewellery and fastened their cloaks with exquisite ornamental brooches.

The Anglo-Saxon women were responsible for making the clothes. Small bronze workboxes found in their graves held needles, thread, and other sewing and weaving implements. The boxes were small enough to be portable, hung from a belt or carried in a pocket.

HOMES   A reconstruction of an Anglo-Saxon hut, based on findings of an excavation, is at the British Museum. It was a simple, crude, one-room affair, about 20 feet long by 12 feet wide. A loom and fragments of pots were found on what must have been a hearth. The hut might have been a workshop, or perhaps the home of a poor family. Excavations of Anglo-Saxon huts have turned up curious discoveries. The skeleton of a middle-aged man, covered with only a thin layer of clay, was found buried in a living room, a knife and comb beside him. In another hut, a dog had been buried.

The study of place names provides clues about the nature of Anglo-Saxon settlements. The ending *ing*, for instance, denotes a group of settlers. It might have been a patronymic, so that the group in a place called Notting would be the family or the sons of Nott, and Nottingham, the home of the family of Nott. It is not agreed that *ing* was a patronymic; it might merely have signified a group, related or not. If a place has the ending *stead* or *fold*, it was probably the place where the outlying buildings were. The ending *worth* or *cot* indicates areas that were somewhat isolated from the main community. *Ton* or *tun* indicates an enclosed agricultural settlement. A *tun* might have had a hall belonging to a thane, on a smaller scale than that of a king.

Of the thousands of place names from Saxon times, comparatively few bear pagan traces. *Har-*

row, from Old English *hearg*, meant sacred place; *wig* or *weoh* meant idol. Nearly all of the Germanic gods were ignored with the exception of Woden and Thunor, commemorated in only fifteen place names. Possibly the heathen gods lost their importance when the settlers came to England. Anglo-Saxon charms, although mingled with Christian ideas, reflect the old superstitions.

The pagan Anglo-Saxon period did not come to an immediate end with the arrival of St. Augustine in 597, but it was not long before the inhabitants of England accepted the teachings of the Christian church. Christianity had been preached in Ireland before the coming of the Germanic tribes, and that branch of the church, known as the Celtic, had to be reconciled to the English one. In 643, the Synod of Whitby brought the two branches together. Eventually they built monasteries where learning and culture were brought to a high level.

Bede completed his history of the church in 731. For a short period there was peace in England, and energies and thoughts were turned to creative work. But the Viking raids, starting in the late eighth century, became a serious threat between 835 and 878. Monasteries were destroyed, and the level of culture declined. Although King Alfred managed, after considerable effort, to maintain a limited peace with the Danes, and to revive interest in learning and education, the raids started again in 980 after a short peaceful period. The Danes held the English throne from 1016 to 1042. Although the English were again restored to the throne, it was only temporary, and the coming of the Normans in 1066 marked the last time that England was invaded.

The findings at Sutton Hoo attest that the heathen Germanic tribes who took over England in the fifth century had achieved a considerable degree of sophistication, and that England, at that early period, was not an isolated, barbaric land. No other excavation of a burial in England approaches the scale and complexity of that at Sutton Hoo. What beliefs did the Anglo-Saxons hold about the world beyond that motivated such a burial? What fears or hopes for the soul of their dead leader compelled his family and followers to honor him with such vast wealth? A burial on that scale must certainly have been known for miles around; why did no one in that age dare to plunder the grave for its priceless treasure? Imagine the preparations, the gathering of the treasure, the strength, ingenuity, and skill required to maneuver that huge ship up a 100-foot slope and across half a mile of land to lower it perfectly into its grave. What ceremony, dances, songs, chants, prayers accompanied this rite? We have only one document that hints of a similar funeral rite—a passage in *Beowulf* that describes the ship-burial of a king.

Excavating the Burial Chamber

Piles of gleaming gold, precious
Gems, scattered on the floor, cups
And bracelets, rusty old helmets, beautifully
Made but rotting with no hands to rub
And polish them.

BEOWULF: 2758–2762

The custom of ship-burial was a pagan one, its purpose to provide the dead with a means of travel on the journey to the world beyond. The kind of ship used, the size, the accompanying regalia, suited the status of the dead. Considering that the Anglo-Saxons had migrated from northern Germany and Denmark, where boat-burials were numerous, it is strange that they have been so rare in Anglo-Saxon archaeology. When the excavators at Sutton Hoo realized the size of the ship, they knew the burial was for someone of high rank.

The burial chamber, roughly in the center of the ship, was 17.5 feet long. It probably looked like a small house—as Mr. Phillips has described it, a bit like Noah's Ark. But at some point, perhaps many years after the burial, the roof collapsed from the weight of the sand, much of it rotted away, and the task of clearing the entire, collapsed, disintegrated mass without treading on treasure was extremely difficult. On top of the burial chamber the excavators came upon a shallow clay pan, 3 feet long by 18 inches wide and 5 inches deep. It appeared to be naturally laminated clay—that is, it had not been baked, but had been hollowed out. Its use remains a mystery, but speculation suggests that it might have served as part of the burial ritual.

Mr. Phillips had to determine how to continue removing earth without a cave-in, and without damaging objects below. He used an ordinary coal shovel mounted on the end of a long handle, and thus, standing off from the burial chamber, he was able to reach over and skim the earth little by little, as though skimming gravy. A pile of earth was building up, nevertheless, endangering their work. Mr. Phillips tried to avoid a cave-in by clearing a wide walk-way at original ground level on either side of the trench. The task of clearing filled-in sand from the bow and stern was a very delicate operation and required the greatest care. The weight of the fill had firmly pressed the ship into its bed. Eventually the wood had disintegrated, but the loose sand that had filled the ship had to be dug out until they reached the firm impression, then gently brushed away. Mr. Phillips credits luck and favorable weather conditions with the prevention of a cave-in. Had there been heavy rains or severe winds, the problems might have been insuperable.

As word of the dig spread, a team of distinguished archaeologists joined Mr. Phillips, eager to help in the excavation.* They were approaching what would have been the floor of the burial chamber when some objects came into view. These objects appeared to be parts of the construction of the chamber: iron spikes, a rusted angle-iron, not unlike two pieces found at Snape, and a bit of decayed oak that could not be identified. Tension mounted. They could not hurry, or the entire treasure would be trod upon and crushed. Yet, with the outbreak of war imminent, there was little time to stop and make careful studies, or to devise some mechanical device that would enable them to continue work without harming objects. Luck and ingenuity

* Professor W. F. Grimes, Professor Stuart Piggot, Mrs. Margaret Guido, Dr. J. B. Ward Perkins, Mr. J. W. Brailsford, Dr. O. G. S Crawford. Photographs were taken by Miss M. Lack and Miss B. Wagstaff, A.R.P.S.

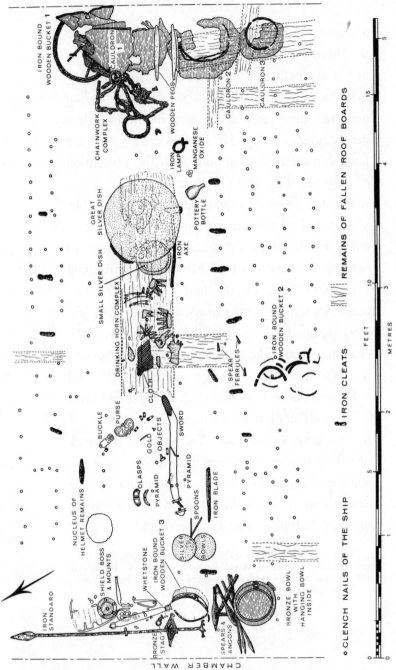

Plan of the burial deposit.
(Based on that of C. W. Phillips, F.S.A.,
ANTIQUARIES JOURNAL, XX, 1940, Plate XXXVII.)

played key roles. Mr. Phillips determined that the treasure was arranged in the shape of an H with a long crossbar, and the two areas on either side of the crossbar relatively open, so that they could move about without damaging objects. (See diagram.) Working on that plan, they went ahead with the dig.

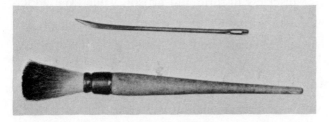

Bodkin and brush used during excavation.

Once the bulk of the fill had been removed, they worked slowly, with knife blades, an assortment of brushes, and blunt probes. Photographic records were kept at each step. Clearing the stern end of the burial chamber, they found the first piece of treasure. Mrs. Guido picked up a small object and brushed it off, revealing a piece of gold jewellery. It was a gold pyramid which would have been attached to a sword-knot, beautifully wrought in an unusual cloisonné technique, and in absolutely perfect condition. In workmanship and perfection of design, it was unlike anything that had ever been found from the Anglo-Saxon period.

During the week of July 26 the main contents of the burial chamber were uncovered. "Each day of that exciting week yielded some first-rate find, often of a type unknown before. As we worked along the keel we *knew* that under those mouldy-looking lumps of decayed wood lay hidden things of priceless historic and artistic value. We anticipated the finding of a sword, shield, helmet, and drinking-horns, and we were not disappointed. Things we did not expect were found—the purse, silver bowls and tray, for instance, and later the axe and suit of chain mail. It was clear that more would be found when the final examination in the laboratories of the British Museum was completed." *

One of the first finds was an iron spike 6 feet 4 inches long, with a square iron grille 11 inches from the tip. It was extremely corroded and fragile, making it difficult to remove. The excavators thought at first it was a flambeau, but further study revealed it to be a standard. A beautifully modeled bronze stag had separated from the top and was found elsewhere. The standard was used as a symbol of sovereignty.**

* O. G. S. Crawford, *Antiquity*, March, 1940, p. 3.
** A description of the individual finds and their historical significance is given in Chapter Two.

1: The Dig

*Bronze Coptic bowl with drop handles, and complex of spears, as uncovered
by excavators. The bronze hanging bowl is inside the Coptic bowl.*

The remains of an iron-bound wooden bucket lay near two bronze bowls, one of which was a Coptic bowl, the other a beautiful hanging bowl. At the time of the excavation the archaeologists could tell very little about them; the bowls were nested one inside the other, with several iron objects close by. Three angons had actually been pushed right through the handle of the larger bowl. Nearby were spearheads and other implements. All these metals were very fragile and much corroded. Some of them had actually corroded together so that it was risky to try to separate them on the site, and the entire complex had to be removed intact without the contents being studied. When the hanging bowl was examined in the British Museum Laboratory, fragments of a six-stringed musical instrument were found in it. After careful examination and study, an instrument has been reconstructed, believed to be like the one that had been in the bowl.

Near the standard, parallel to it, was a whetstone, a formidable-looking object two feet long, weighing almost six and a half pounds, with four savage faces carved at each end.

The next complex of objects was so disintegrated and confused that it was difficult to identify anything at first glance. It became apparent that the

Fragments of maplewood and metal fittings from the musical instrument.

remains of a shield lay there because a decorative iron shield-boss and shield-mounts were visible. As they removed the objects, fragments of gold leaf blew away in the wind.* The shield had been made of wood, now totally disintegrated, which had been covered with leather and decorated with highly wrought metal mounts, some in the form of a bird- or dragon-head.

Near the shield were the fragments of a helmet. Despite its shattered condition and the fact that the pieces had been scattered by the weight of the falling roof, certain features were recognizable, particularly the bronze face-piece consisting of a life-size nose and mouth, complete with a neatly clipped moustache. By now it was evident that the excavators had come upon the grave of a high-ranking warrior, doubtless a king. The entire west end of the chamber was reserved for arms. But so far, they had found no evidence of the remains of a body.

They uncovered a large lump of purple earth, about the size of a man's head. The color indicated the presence of silver—corroded silver turns to silver chloride, which is purple. Undercutting the

* Mr. Phillips states in a private letter: "It is my own conviction that this represents the gold leaf which had probably been applied all over the front of the shield." During the work of taking the mold in 1967, gold leaf continued to fly about.

earth around the lump, they wedged a large iron
plate beneath so that it could be removed in its
entirety without disturbing the contents. It was set
aside while the excavators went on with the work
of removing the jewellery.

Finding the sword-knots had prepared them
for the extraordinary hoard of gold jewellery, although they could not have anticipated the quantity. A large gold buckle, intricately wrought,
gleaming gold, weighing nearly a pound, was one
of the most striking pieces. Except for this and
one or two other items, all the gold pieces were
jeweled with garnets. A purse, elegant in design,
unique of its kind, was called "the most gorgeous
of the finds," by Dr. Bruce-Mitford. It contained
37 gold coins.

In the area with the gold jewellery lay a sword,
nearly three feet long, buried in its scabbard. Badly
corroded, sword and scabbard will remain forever
rusted and inseparable. The pommel is gold with
gold filigree mounts on the hilt, and ornamental
scabbard-bosses.

Local gossip was beginning to spread, and there
were curiosity seekers, as well as the expected interruptions from the press. And of course, distinguished visitors arrived, eager to learn about the
excavation. It meant constant interruptions. In ad-

dition, security was a problem, since the value of the treasure was inestimable. It was difficult to keep secret a find in which work was carried out in the open. One evening, upon returning to the hotel, Professor Piggot was jokingly asked by one of the local Woodbridge citizens, "Find any gold today?" "My pockets are full of it," Professor Piggot replied. The citizens of Woodbridge looked upon the archaeologists with tolerant amusement, and perhaps regarded their work as a waste of time.*

Another difficulty was packing and preserving the finds, already fragmented and corroded, in order to send them to the laboratory for study. Some items could not survive any prolonged exposure and had to be swiftly immersed in water until moist packing could be found. With so little time to arrange for equipment, Mr. Phillips and his crew had to improvise. The nearby woods supplied damp moss, ideal for packing. By keeping basins of water at hand, and quantities of the soft, damp moss, they could pack and protect the fragmented objects. The local grocers and chemists at Woodbridge provided cotton wool, boxes, string, and jars. Mrs. Pretty supplied tea towels. Some objects with hard

* The most recent Woodbridge guide issued by the Town Council in the spring of 1968 has no mention at all of the Sutton Hoo mounds.

*Archaeologists examining material found under the large silver dish.
C. W. Phillips is on the left, W. F. Grimes is next to him.
A grid, used to chart the relative position of objects before
they are removed from the earth, is in the upper left corner.*

sand tightly packed around them simply remained in their enclosure until they reached the laboratory. A record was kept of each day's work: a careful description of each item and its exact location were noted before it was hurriedly packed in moss. How Mr. Phillips managed this in the midst of the excitement and the interruptions, with time at his back, is a miracle of patience and organization.

The crew, busy packing and recording, had forgotten the purple lump until late in the day someone noticed it when it suddenly moved. It seemed to heave, as though drawing a breath, and with a loud metallic click, it broke apart. There, in the earth, lay six beautiful silver bowls. The bright afternoon sun had dried the damp sand, causing the tightly packed bowls to spring apart. Ten silver bowls had been nested together and placed upside down in the grave. The two top ones had totally disintegrated to silver chloride, two others were damaged, but six, protected by the others, were perfect.

At this point Mr. Phillips thought it important that the site be visited by Mr. T. D. Kendrick, at the time Keeper of British and Medieval Antiquities at the British Museum. Mr. Phillips knew that no description of the finds could convey the beauty of the jewellery, so he decided that the best way to prepare Mr. Kendrick for what he would see at the site would be to take one of the choice pieces of jewellery with him when he went to the station to meet Mr. Kendrick's train. Mr. Phillips chose a small gold buckle inlaid with jewels, which he packed in a tobacco tin and carried in his pocket. When the train pulled into the station and Mr. Kendrick stepped down, Mr. Phillips led the authority from the British Museum into the waiting room, where he opened the tobacco tin and revealed its gleaming contents.

Near the nest of silver bowls two silver rods were found that proved, upon examination, to be spoons, well preserved, with graceful fig-shaped bowls. The niello inscription on the long rods read "Saulos" and "Paulos," indicating that they were Christian objects, perhaps a conversion gift, amidst the trappings of what was essentially a pagan burial.

The central section of the burial chamber contained all the personal possessions of the dead warrior. The west end appeared to be the area for official regalia to signify status. If there had been a body, it would have lain in the central chamber, but so far, although all the strap-mounts that would have been worn by the warrior were found, no trace of a body was visible. The central section also held items used for feasting, such as drinking horns, and tiny cups that might have been for stronger drink.

*C. W. Phillips lifting the large silver dish, twenty-eight inches in diameter.
Under it, textiles, leather, and other articles were found.
W. F. Grimes is on the right.*

The horns had disintegrated and only the shattered remains of the silver mounts were found.

One of the most unusual finds in this area was an enormous silver platter that had been placed covering other objects, almost as though it were a blanket, the sides tucked and bent around the treasures beneath. From the shape and size, the excavators thought it was a shield, but immediately realized that a wooden shield would not have survived. Beneath this dish was a smaller silver dish with a female head in the style of classical Greece embossed in the center. An afternoon and evening were spent removing the entire complex. Some preparatory work had been done the previous morning to determine whether the dish could be removed in its entirety, and it was found, despite surface corrosion and a crack along the side, to be quite strong. After the dish was removed, the assortment of organic materials beneath demanded immediate attention; the slightest delay would cause disintegration. The excavators found the remains of a leather bag, several pairs of leather shoes, two bone combs, some flock-like material that may have been the stuffing of a pillow, and some bits of cloth. At the bottom was a mass of rusted chain mail.

At the east end of the burial chamber were placed objects for domestic use. Amidst this complex were three wooden pegs, each about 18 inches long; why they survived when all other wood in the chamber had rotted is not clear. Nor is it clear what they were used for. Possibly they had a practical use in engineering the ship into position,* or they may have been scraps of wood left behind by those who built the burial chamber.

Throughout the excavation the members of the crew were careful to watch for traces of either cremation or inhumation, but no trace of a body was ever found. The conclusion is that the grave had been a cenotaph to honor a great man, doubtless a king, whose body for some reason could not be recovered for burial. The questions of who he was and what happened to his body are still being debated.

The excavators were nearing the end of their work. During the last week of July, newspapers all over the world announced the finding of the Sutton Hoo treasure. But did the treasure belong to Mrs. Pretty, on whose land it was found, or was it the property of the Crown? On August 14 a coroner's inquest was held at which it was decided that the objects were not Treasure Trove—that is, the treas-

* A description of Mr. Phillips' speculation as to how the ship was lowered into position is given in Chapter Two.

ure had originally been buried with no intent to recover it—and Mrs. Pretty was therefore the legal owner.* If the Nation wanted it, it would have to buy it—at what price, no one could imagine. Nine days later, Mrs. Pretty announced that she would give the entire treasure to the Nation.

The treasure was sent to the British Museum, where the fragile objects were treated in the laboratory. Then everything was removed to a bomb-proof hiding place. Scholars had no time to study the finds; the public had to await the end of the war before the treasure could be placed on view at the Museum. The archaeologists who had worked on the dig and who, doubtless, realized as they completed their task that military service would be their next assignment, went immediately to war. By September 1, six days after the excavators had completed their work, the exciting story of finding the grave of an Anglo-Saxon king was overshadowed by the news of the outbreak of World War II. Once again the treasure at Sutton Hoo sank into obscurity.

* Further discussion of the legal decision will be found in Chapter Four.

CHAPTER TWO

THE TREASURE

Putting the Pieces Together in the
British Museum Laboratory

Come, let us enter the tower, see
The dragon's marvelous treasure one
Last time: I'll lead the way, take you
Close to that heap of curious jewels,
And rings, and gold.

BEOWULF: 3101–3105

Introduction

THE FUNDAMENTALS of archaeology cannot be condensed in a chapter, or even in one book. Webster defines archaeology as "the scientific study of the life and culture of ancient peoples, as by excavation of ancient cities, relics, artifacts, etc." But an artifact has no historical value until it can be identified and placed in time. Thus, the archaeologist's concern is not merely with finding relics, but with finding out about them. He must not only know techniques of excavation, but he must have a thorough knowledge of the history and the language of the people and the period he is studying. A specialist in classical archaeology, for instance, might know how to conduct an excavation in Mexico, or England—exactly how to approach a site so as to prevent damage to objects, how to take notes with diagrams and maps—but he would probably know very little about what he found.

Anglo-Saxon archaeology has been called "the Cinderella among antiquarian studies," * simply because there are so few Anglo-Saxon archaeologists, and those few have had to learn their subject through a study of related fields. There have been scarcely any university courses in Anglo-Saxon archaeology.

One of the difficulties in Anglo-Saxon archaeology is that the exact chronology of pagan Anglo-Saxon England has not been established; only with historical evidence is it possible to establish absolute dating of finds. In the absence of historical evidence, an object can be dated if, for instance, the name of an historical figure is inscribed on it, if it has been found in the grave of a known person, or if it has been found with other datable finds, such as coins. When an object can be dated within narrow limits, other similar objects can be dated by using the object whose date is known as a guide. Thus, a *relative* chronology may be established even when no absolute date can be arrived at. The archaeologist goes about establishing a relative chronology in detective fashion: he finds as much evidence as pos-

* D. M. Wilson, *The Anglo-Saxons*, Thames and Hudson, London, 1960, p. 16.

sible, studies it, compares it with other available evidence, and, above all, works closely with all available historical documents. In the case of the Sutton Hoo finds, the historical document most closely related to them is the poem *Beowulf*, which itself has not been precisely dated. The problem of dating the Sutton Hoo finds accurately has been compounded by the fact that the burial chamber contained many antiques, or family heirlooms, some of them imported, and by the fact that the Merovingian coins are extremely difficult to date. "The time will come when a relative chronology can be erected for the whole of the Anglo-Saxon period on a basis acceptable to both the statistician and the historian. With the aid of new scientific methods, such as dendrochronology (tree-ring dating) and radio-carbon dating techniques, it may even be possible within the next fifty years to build up a reasonably accurate chronology." *

Few archaeological finds have the enormous intrinsic value of those at Sutton Hoo. The abundance of gold, garnet, and silver revealed for the first time the level of wealth and the scale of life of an East Anglian king in the seventh century, and in all probability the treasure represents only a small

* *Ibid.*, p. 22.

portion of the royal treasury.

Most archaeological finds consist of fragments of pottery, stone carvings, jewels, bone, metal, remains of buildings, or ordinary household utensils —all of which are important in adding to our knowledge of the past. Such fragments can easily be destroyed by treasure hunters searching only for valuables, or by archaeologists with clumsy excavating techniques.

An experienced archaeologist can determine some facts about his finds while he is in the field. The size and shape of an object made of leather, bone, ivory, or any other material that disintegrates, can often be determined by the remaining ornamental framework, or mounts. A photograph of the mounts taken *in situ* serves as a guide for the laboratory scientist in reconstructing disintegrated objects. The analysis and preservation of art objects is a comparatively new science, and techniques for preservation and reconstruction have improved vastly in recent years. The chief value of the Sutton Hoo ship-burial is, in Dr. Bruce-Mitford's words, that "it is the first royal grave of this era in Europe to have come down to modern times unburnt and unrobbed, to have been recorded in detail by modern archaeological science and photography, and to have applied to its definition, elucidation, and re-

The helmet reconstructed, front view.

construction from the first the resources of modern laboratory technique and of modern comparative research." *

The Helmet

Glittering at the top
Of their golden helmets wild boar heads gleamed,
Shining decorations, swinging as they marched,
Erect like guards, like sentinels, as though ready
To fight.

BEOWULF: 303–306

"On the north side of the keel-line and about 3 or 4 feet out from the west wall of the chamber were many small corroded and fragile fragments of a shattered iron helmet." ** When these fragments were unpacked in the British Museum Laboratory, they covered the top of what was described as "a good-sized table." †

It took Mr. Maryon, in the British Museum Lab-

* R. L. S. Bruce-Mitford, "The Sutton Hoo Ship-Burial," Appendix in R. H. Hodgkin, *A History of the Anglo-Saxons*, Oxford University Press, London, 1952, p. 728.
** R. L. S. Bruce-Mitford, *The Sutton Hoo Ship-Burial: A Handbook*, The British Museum, London, 1968, p. 27.
† Herbert Maryon, "The Sutton Hoo Helmet," *Antiquity*, September, 1947, p. 137.

62

oratory, six months of continuous full-time work to recreate the helmet from the mass of fragments. The burial-chamber roof had collapsed on the helmet after it had already rusted, and there the remains had lain amidst sand and decaying timber for centuries. Recognizable were the distinct nose, mouth, and moustache; two gilded bronze dragon-heads were also clearly distinguishable, but the rest —three or four hundred bits encrusted with sand and rust—had little resemblance to anything but scraps from a junk heap. On some pieces, however, faint traces of a design could be discerned.

Mr. Maryon set to work sorting the fragments. He placed each fragile scrap on a piece of stiff cardboard, which facilitated handling and provided a convenient means of drawing an outline of each fragment, as well as a place to note any outstanding details such as a distinct design. Before he made an attempt at reconstruction, he spent a long period studying and comparing fragments.

The helmet had been made of sheet iron, the surface of which was covered with sheets of thin, tinned bronze that had been stamped with embossed designs. The method believed to have been used to make these designs is described by Mr. Maryon and consisted of making a die or pattern, of a design and then hammering the pattern onto the bronze sheet, which had a tin wash on one side and was protected with a piece of lead on the other while the design was hammered in.

As the work progressed, a distinct figure of a warrior, similar to figures that had been noted on helmets found in Sweden from the Vendel period (A.D. 600–800), became recognizable. Bit by bit, designs on the panels began to emerge. Mr. Maryon found that nature had been cooperative, for in some cases the slow accumulation of iron rust that covered the pieces had "deposited a clean layer of brown hematite,* free from grit. It was a deposit of this nature that I found: a mould formed by nature reproducing the ornament which otherwise would have been lost forever where the bronze plaque decayed." ** Since the iron foundation and the embossed covering were nearly totally disintegrated, Mr. Maryon cleaned and oiled the surface of the mold, reinforced the back with plaster, and then made a plaster-of-Paris cast. When he finished this work on one of the fragments, part of a figure was revealed, a human figure with legs in mid-air. As Mr. Maryon continued to work, various parts of the design came into view until he had almost a complete picture: a figure on horseback is riding

* Hematite is iron ore.
** Maryon, "The Sutton Hoo Helmet," pp. 138–39.

down another warrior wearing a coat of mail who has fallen. The design on some of the fragments was so unclear that Mr. Maryon had to guess where to place them. One design that appeared to show warriors in horned helmets puzzled Mr. Maryon until

Dancing warriors from the Sutton Hoo helmet.

Dr. Bruce-Mitford, during a visit to the Uppland province of Sweden, observed similar designs on a panel of a helmet from Valsgarde, a place where Viking and pre-Viking ship-burials have been found. With the help of the model, it became apparent that the two figures were doing a ritual sword dance. Another panel has a design that reveals only part of a leg; the rest of the design is lost. After the helmet was reconstructed, Mr. Maryon found that it was divided into panels, some of which were stamped with figures in a repeated motif or in an interlace ornamental design to make an over-all pattern. Some figures appear to be in combat: others are doing a ritual dance.

The size of the helmet resembles those worn by motorcyclists, with space between the wearer's head and the crown for protective padding. A crest inlaid with silver wires runs from between the eyebrows, across the top of the crown, to the nape of the neck, with garnet-eyed dragon heads at either end. This kind of helmet was described in *Beowulf*, but the lines were never fully understood until piecing together the Sutton Hoo helmet helped to clarify them.

> The helmet's
> Brim was wound with bands of metal,
> Rounded ridges to protect whoever

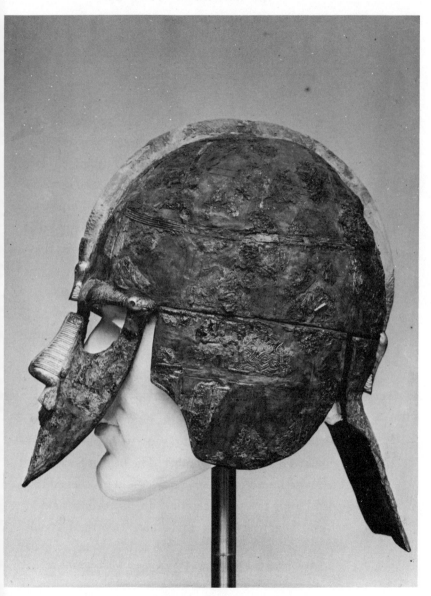

Helmet, side view.

Wore it from swords swung in the fiercest
Battles, shining iron edges
In hostile hands.

This reinforced brim served as added protection to the wearer, enabling him to sustain heavy blows on top of his helmet. The eyebrows terminated in gilt-bronze boar-heads, which probably also served as protection. The *Beowulf* poet described a boar-image on top of the helmet (see quote at opening of this chapter), but this was not a feature of the Sutton Hoo helmet.*

In order to assemble the fragments into an actual helmet, Mr. Maryon first made a plaster model of an average head. Then he made a padding over the crown, where the protective material would have been, so that he could approximate the size, and finally he stuck each piece of the helmet into the plaster model. When all the fragments had been arranged, he filled in any gaps with plaster and covered it with brown umber. The helmet is similar to those found in Swedish graves and is believed to date from the sixth century. In its reconstructed form, it appears quite drab, but, as Mr. Maryon

* According to Dr. Bruce-Mitford, there will be revisions in the reconstruction of the helmet.

pointed out, "we have to imagine it in its original condition as an object of burnished silvery metal, set in a trellis-work of gold, surmounted by a crest of massive silver, and embellished with gilded ornaments, garnets and niello—in its way a magnificent thing and one of the outstanding masterpieces of barbaric art." *

Hrothgar's helmet would defend him;
That ancient, shining treasure, encircled
With hard-rolled metal, set there by some smith's
Long dead hand, would block all battle
Swords, stop all blades from cutting at him.

BEOWULF: 1448–1452

The Jewellery

Silver and jewels buried in the sandy
Ground, back in the earth again
And forever hidden and useless to men.

BEOWULF: 3166–3168

The perfection of the gold jewellery is overwhelming. Thousands of garnets have been individually cut in the most intricate patterns, combined

* Maryon, "The Sutton Hoo Helmet," p. 144.

with millefiori enamel in blue and white or red, and set in gold. Approximately 26 individual pieces of gold jewellery were found in the center of the burial chamber along the keel-line, within an area 3 feet by 3 feet by 6 inches. Many pieces were found face down and appeared to be in no particular arrangement. The perfection of the workmanship has convinced archaeologists that the jewellery was created by "one of the greatest goldsmiths ever produced by the early Germanic world." *

The purse lid is of gold, garnet, and millefiori decorative designs. These designs had been set in bone or ivory, which has now disintegrated, and the entire lid was set in a jewelled gold frame. It is believed that the top of the purse was attached to the wearer's belt straps by three gold hinges, since a simple but effective sliding catch is at the bottom of the lid. The purse contained 37 gold coins, two gold ingots, and three coin-size blank flans.

The gold buckle, more than five inches long and weighing more than 14 ounces, is beautifully wrought with designs of intricate interlace patterns and niello inlay. Although the style is similar to work done in Sweden, historians believe that it is of English make because the design resembles other

* R. L. S. Bruce-Mitford, in R. H. Hodgkin, *A History of the Anglo-Saxons*, p. 706.

Gold buckle, enlarged approximately one and a half times.

Anglo-Saxon pieces. The buckle is different from the other pieces of jewellery in composition—that is, the gold is paler, and so is judged to contain about 13 percent silver. The other gold pieces contain only about 2 percent. Sliding catches on the back attached to the wearer's belt. Mr. Phillips described it as "an ostentatious piece of such weight that it must have been an embarrassment to its wearer." *

The curved panels of the unique shoulder clasps are perfect in design, done in an over-all carpet-like pattern in cloisonné and millefiori. The borders are gold, fashioned in a lovely interlace pattern, and each end has a striking animal design interwoven with large pieces of garnet. Most remarkable is the delicate and decorative fastening pin attached by a gold chain. When the pin is pulled out, the hinges separate into two parts. The clasps were worn on the shoulders, forming part of a leather harness.

Several other smaller pieces excavated formed either parts of the harness or parts of the decorative fittings for the sword belt. The excavators believed that the leather harness to which the strap-mounts were attached had originally been suspended from the roof. Dr. Ortwin Gamber attempted to assemble

* C. W. Phillips, *Antiquaries Journal*, April, 1940, p. 167.

One of the pair of shoulder clasps with garnet and enamel cloisonné decoration.

the strap-mounts and buckles in the way in which they might have been distributed when the warrior was in full dress. He based his conclusions on how warriors of the period were believed to have dressed. Then he studied the position in which the strap-mounts were found in the grave and tested his theory on a dummy.

Seven of the larger mounts were distributed along a belt, to decorate it and to prevent it from twisting. Smaller mounts may have been placed on a narrower belt, perhaps a sword strap. Then the purse was attached to the waist-belt by loops. Dr. Gamber placed the heavy gold buckle as a terminal on a linen band strapped around the chest. In this position the buckle served a purely decorative function. Dr. Gamber gave the following description of the way the Sutton Hoo warrior might have looked in his parade dress:

The under-garment . . . and the band . . . were invariably white, the shield, cloak, stockings and shoes were red, the leather straps and scabbard were red or white. The cuirass . . . was either red or purple (or in this case perhaps dark-blue). As the strap-mounts from Sutton Hoo are red, one can expect that the cuirass would be dyed either purple or dark blue, when the blue-enamelled parts of the mounts would have harmonized well. The helmet and shield-boss were usually silvered, while nearly all other parts were enriched with decoration in gold. The whole outfit was therefore based on the colour combination of white or silver and red or purple (dark blue) with gold, a combination that corresponded to the medieval vestments of the Emperor and doubtless derived from Roman tradition.

The appearance of the fully-armed king must have been one of barbaric but nevertheless of most impressive splendour. There can be little doubt that the Sutton Hoo equipment should be regarded as regalia rather than a military outfit, although in case of necessity it might be used as the latter: it corresponds to the dress of the Roman Emperor as commander-in-chief in the official portraits which extend from Augustus to Theodosius.*

Despite being buried for 1300 years, all hinges and moving parts of the jewellery worked perfectly. All of the jewellery had been made by hand,

* Ortwin Gamber, "The Sutton Hoo Military Equipment—an Attempted Reconstruction," *The Journal of The Arms and Armour Society*, June, 1966, pp. 285–86.

and it must have taken many years. There are 4000 individually cut garnets set in the 26 or so pieces of jewellery; even working parts of hinges have been studded with garnets. Because these stones are brittle, there is often much waste in cutting. Even using present-day equipment, a skilled stonecutter takes a full day to finish cutting a simple stone and two or three days for the more intricately cut stones. Probably the Sutton Hoo jewellery was made in the workshop of one master craftsman. Archaeologists believe that the mushroom design, worked repeatedly into the over-all pattern, served as the artist's signature. Animal designs have been used over and over, as though the artist preferred those forms.

"The gold jewellery is brimming with novel and daring ideas. It shows an overflowing exuberance and displays the highest level of craftsmanship excelling anything known in this medium from the rest of Europe in its era." *

The Standard and Whetstone

Healfdane's son gave Beowulf a golden
Banner, a fitting flag to signal

* R. L. S. Bruce-Mitford, *The Sutton Hoo Ship-Burial*, p. 73.

His victory, and gave him, as well, a helmet,
And a coat of mail, and an ancient sword.

BEOWULF: 1020–1023

When the 6-foot 4-inch standard was found, it was thought at first to be a portable flambeau, although nothing is known of methods of lighting during the Anglo-Saxon period. The delicate task of lifting it was accomplished by carefully under-cutting and wedging a long, heavy board beneath, and supporting the find with cotton packing so that three men could lift out the entire object. Although nothing resembling the standard has ever been found, several references to standards occur in Anglo-Saxon literature, and references to golden standards occur in *Beowulf*.

The Sutton Hoo standard has an iron grille eleven inches from the top, the purpose of which has not yet been determined. Perhaps it held flags or gold-embroidered banners or wreaths or some other decorative but perishable attachment. The stag atop the standard, thought at first to belong to the helmet, was beautifully made, and may have some association with the cult of Woden, from whom the East Anglian royal family supposedly derived. It is similar to a stag from the third millennium B.C. found in a royal tomb in Anatolia in Asia Minor, and it has been conjectured that it might be an

77

Bronze stag from the top of the standard.

antique from the Middle East.*

The presence of the standard and whetstone affirms that this was a royal burial. These objects were symbols of sovereignty, probably used in ceremonies and rituals of which no record exists. Bede referred to a standard associated with King Edwin (616–33):

> The king's dignity was highly respected throughout his realm, and whether in battle or on a peaceful progress through city, town, and countryside in the company of his thanes, the royal standard was always borne before him. And whenever he passed through the streets on foot, the standard known to the Romans as *Tufa,* and to the English as a *Tuf,* was also carried in front of him.**

The whetstone showed no signs of use and is believed to have had a function in the ceremonial rites attending a king. It is two feet long, weighs six and a half pounds, and has four fierce human faces carved at each end. Three of the four faces at one end are bearded and appear to be masculine, the four at the other end appear to be feminine. Atop

---

* In a letter to the author from Dr. R. L. S. Bruce-Mitford.
** Bede, *A History of the English Church and People,* translated by Leo Sherley-Price, Penguin Books, Baltimore, 1955, p. 130.

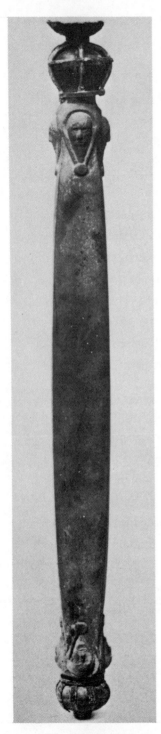

The whetstone.   Whetstone (detail).

Whetstone: Bearded head (detail).

each set of faces is a knob painted red. An American scholar who has studied the whetstone has noted parallels with other early artifacts of the four-headed symbol, which seem to depict the god looking out to the four points of the compass. He finds this to be one of several indications that the whetstone is associated with the cult of Thor.*

The Musical Instrument and Bronze Bowls

As day after day the music rang
Loud in that hall, the harp's rejoicing
Call and the poet's clear songs, sung
Of the ancient beginnings of us all.

BEOWULF: 88–91

Near the standard the excavators found a large bronze bowl with another smaller bowl nested inside it. The larger bowl was made with simple fluting and animal engraving on the inside. It had drop handles, and has been identified as a Coptic bowl.** The smaller bowl, quite damaged, proved to be the remains of a Celtic hanging bowl. It was

* Sidney L. Cohen, "The Sutton Hoo Whetstone." *Speculum*, July, 1966.
** Similar bowls have been found in burials in various parts of the continent. Another Coptic bowl was found in the Taplow burial in England, a rich seventh century burial.

ABOVE   *Hanging bowl. The circular enameled escutcheons are red and blue.*
Rotating fish on pedestal is in the center of the bowl.
BELOW   *Rotating bronze fish on pedestal from the interior of the large*
hanging bowl. The fish had been spotted with sunken enamel studs.
The fins and tail have been damaged.

decorated with eight enameled escutcheons, or medallions; the center one at the bottom of the bowl
served as a support for a rotating bronze fish, identified as a trout, on a pedestal. The use of the bowl
has not been determined. The presence of the fish, a
Christian symbol, has led to the conjecture that
such bowls were used in Celtic Christian churches.
The bowl showed signs of having been repaired
and patched in several places by Saxon craftsmen.
Of the seventy or more bowls found in England
which date from the fifth to seventh centuries, the
Sutton Hoo bowl was the most elaborately decorated. The Saxon tribes may have looted it from the
native population.

At the time of the excavation, shafts of iron
throwing-spears were found thrust through the
handles, and iron-socketed spearheads were inter-
mingled with the bowls. This complex had to be
moved to the laboratory without further examination. When the bowls and iron objects were sorted,
the remains of a musical instrument were found in
the smaller bowl. When the fragments of wood
were laid out, they appeared as little more than
sweepings from a fireplace, but certain parts had a
recognizable form and were identifiable. Two ten-
on-and-mortise joints of the frame were put together and found to fit two gilt bronze escutcheons.
When scientists detected six holes in what appeared

to be the upper arm of the object and found remains of six pegs, they knew it had been a six-stringed musical instrument. Botanists analyzed the wood: the pegs were either of poplar or of willow, the frame was of maplewood. Following designs worked out by the Museum, a reconstruction was built by Mr. L. Ward in the Workshops of Messrs. Arnold Dolmetsch. The musical instrument that resulted has a light and melodic tone; its design was later confirmed by a drawing found in a twelfth-century manuscript. Since then additional fragments have been sorted out, and with these new pieces further studies will be made.*

The Shield

> They arrived with their mail shirts
> Glittering, silver-shining links
> Clanking an iron song as they came.
> Sea-weary still, they set their broad,
> Battle-hardened shields in rows
> Along the wall.

BEOWULF: 321–326

Except for traces of wood, the shield itself had totally disintegrated. But the excavators recog-

* See Appendix, p. 161.

The shield, reconstructed, front view.

nized that what they had found had been a shield
by the large, heavy iron shield-boss, which would
have been in the center of the shield. Other metal
fittings and ornamental mounts, identified as part of
the shield, were scattered about.

Because the excavators took photographs from
various angles, in order to show the mass exactly as
it lay in the ground, it was possible to reconstruct
the shield. In the laboratory all the elements were
laid out so that the size, shape, and spatial arrange-
ments of the mounts could be determined. At first it
was thought to have been a straight-sided shield, but
that seemed unlikely since shields of that shape
were the product of a period five hundred years
earlier. Further study of sources—the Franks Casket made in Northumbria in the seventh century,
and Scandinavian shields of the same period—
showed that shields made at the time of the Sutton
Hoo burial were round. Mr. Herbert Maryon and
his staff drew these conclusions:

> Consideration of the plan [of the burial
> chamber] showed that two heavy objects—the
> "standard" and the whetstone—lay just along-
> side the shield, and all three lay close to the
> western end of the burial chamber, which,
> after standing for many years, had collapsed

inwards under the pressure of the sand piled against it. It seemed probable that if, by that time, the thin wooden shield had become decayed, the collapse of the wall would have been likely to drive the edge of the shield inwards in the direction of its centre line. A further examination of the photographs enabled us to observe this movement, as it were, actually in progress. The weight of the shield-boss had caused it to sink through the decayed wood of the shield, so that the shield-border, a ring of wood rather more than two inches wide and a little thicker than that of the adjacent parts of the shield, had broken loose and slid forward till it had in fact overhung the wide flange of the shield-boss. As it moved forward it split up into numerous narrow sections, and the photographs show some of these sections moving a little in advance of their neighbours. We found also that the edge of the shield had been strengthened by a U-sectioned bronze binding made from a folded half-inch strip of bronze. This had run right round the shield, protecting and stiffening the edge. This band, decayed and fragmentary though it was, had done something to keep together the broken parts of the edge of the shield, so that they had moved forward more or less as one. Further pieces of evidence convinced us, at last, that the shield had been circular. I give an example of what I mean. The U-shaped band round the shield had been of bronze, covered with gold leaf. A number of short lengths, protected by the gold, remained intact. They were seen to be curved. We drew out on the bench parts of a number of circles of about the same curvature and tried lengths of bronze against them. At 16½ inches radius, or 33 inches diameter, they fitted exactly. Thus our original estimate for the diameter of the shield was confirmed.*

Mr. Maryon and his staff had to determine curvature and thickness before they could begin reconstructing the shield. When they had examined the pieces of the shield-grip (the heavy bar with which the warrior held his shield) and arranged them in place, it appeared that the shield had been slightly curved. A small, but complete, cross-section of the shield had survived. This piece of wood was five sixths of an inch thick, with leather on either side. A portion of the arm-strap—the strap

* Herbert Maryon, "The Sutton Hoo Shield," *Antiquity*, March, 1946, p. 23.

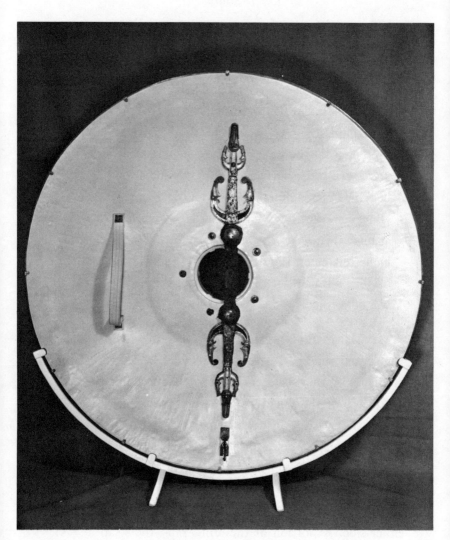

The shield, showing back.

Detail of shield boss.

supporting the warrior's forearm—had also survived.

The central boss of the shield was an imposing object of iron and gilt-bronze, with garnet and niello decoration. Gilt-bronze bird-heads with garnet inlays were evident, as was a bronze-winged dragon that Mr. Maryon believed might have been placed on the shield by a warrior who considered himself equal to Beowulf, the dragon-fighter. Signs of extensive repair made it evident that the shield was old at the time of burial, perhaps one hundred years, or slightly older. Like the helmet and the sword, this weapon was an heirloom, possibly made by Swedish armorers.*

The Drinking Horns

The keeper of the mead
Came carrying out the carved flasks,
And poured that bright sweetness. A poet
Sang, from time to time, in a clear
Pure voice.

BEOWULF: 493–497

Two of the drinking horns found at Sutton Hoo are the largest Anglo-Saxon ones in existence,

---

* The British Museum has began work on a new reconstruction of the shield.

Drinking horns, reconstructed.

boasting a capacity of six quarts. They are 41.5 inches long, with the diameter at the mouth a little more than 7 inches. Seven horns were found; two large ones from the now extinct aurochs, and five smaller horns from cows. The horns had totally disintegrated, but the mass of horn-mounts was photographed *in situ*, then lifted on a glass sheet and placed in a box. A numbered and lettered grid was then fitted over it and photographed, so that the location of each fragment was recorded before the box was transported to the laboratory. There all the fragments were sorted; each one was placed on a separate card and carefully drawn and described. Thus, should further disintegration or damage result, the record is there for reference.

The two large horns had been decorated at the mouth and the tip with silver mounts made of the same die, making them a pair. The five smaller ones were probably a set because they also had decorations made of the same die.

To reconstruct these horns the scientist must work with broken bits, many of which are missing. Although the horns had completely disintegrated, it was possible to determine from the size of the silver mounts how large the horns had been. To reconstruct accurately an aurochs' horn, accounting for the correct shape and curvature and the proper size of mouth opening, an aurochs' skull from the Natural History Museum in London was used, and a plaster mold made of the horn before fastening on the metal mounts. The hunting and slaying of an aurochs was an old custom and, to the Germanic tribes, an important ritual connected with proving manly strength.

The Sword

It had
An iron blade, etched and shining
And hardened in blood. No one who'd worn it
Into battle, swung it in dangerous places,
Daring and brave, had ever been deserted.

BEOWULF: 1457–1461

The sword, with its jeweled gold pommel and scabbard, is one of the few Anglo-Saxon swords found, although swords must have been most important weapons to the Anglo-Saxon. They were usually treasured family heirlooms handed down from father to son, not possessed by every man, but only by those with money and rank. Often a sword was given a name; Beowulf's sword was called *Naegling*.

During the pagan Anglo-Saxon period the sword was about two and one half feet long, thin-bladed, two-edged, called a *spatha*. It was carried in a scabbard, usually ornamented, leather-covered wood, sometimes lined with fleece. The natural oils of the sheep supposedly kept the blade from rusting. Blades either were made of one piece of metal, or they were pattern-welded—that is, twisted iron bands were beaten thin, edged with steel, and then polished, creating a wavy pattern on the blade.

The Sutton Hoo sword, rusted in its scabbard, has been examined by radiography and found to be pattern-welded in a chevron pattern. The blade is 28 inches, a bit shorter than other Anglo-Saxon swords; the over-all length is 2 feet 9 inches. So far as can be determined, the sheath is of wood with leather next to the blade. Four inches from the lower guard are two small round jewelled bosses— actually small buttons—beautifully wrought in a cruciform design of gold cloisonné with garnets. Swedish swords have been found with small scabbard-bosses, but such decorative devices are a rarity on an English sword.

When the Sutton Hoo treasure was examined in the British Museum Laboratory, a lump of sand was found to contain a gilt-bronze ring. The purpose of the ring, like those which are found on

96

LEFT *The sword*
ABOVE *Sword hilt*
BELOW *Scabbard bosses*

ring-swords, is to signify rank. This ring may have been taken from another sword, since no ring-sword was found with the other grave goods.

The Coins

The coins provide the best clue for dating the Sutton Hoo ship-burial, but, as the key factor, they have become the center of some controversy.

Thirty-seven Merovingian coins, three blanks, and two gold ingots were found in the purse. Merovingian France, which comprised modern France, Belgium, Switzerland, and the Rhineland, had numerous mints, since every village could strike coins. The locations of about 2000 of those mints are known. Each Sutton Hoo coin was struck at a different mint.

Merovingian coins are difficult to date. Sometimes the die had been cut incorrectly so that the legend has to be read in reverse. Sometimes these reverse letters are even more difficult to decipher because the small surface of the coin did not take the entire letter. About 30 percent of the Sutton Hoo coins cannot be read with certainty. Only one king has been identified on one of the coins: Theodebert II, a Frankish king who ruled between 595 and 612. Of all the rest, it can only be said that they have a head on one side and a cross on the other.

The most recent study,* which estimates that the Sutton Hoo hoard was assembled between 625 and 630, about fifty years earlier than the previous estimates, has gained general acceptance, although some historians hold to an even later date.**

This hoard of coins was probably not a merchant's hoard. If the coins had been gathered at random through trade and then hoarded for future use, they would not represent such a variety of mints. Was there, in the seventh century, a coin collector who was fascinated by the different coins? Did he want to have the raw materials—the ingots and the flans—as examples of the intermediate stages of coin manufacture?

The Silver

As we watched emerging daily from the earth things that we saw were unique we felt that we were present at the unveiling of history, and

---

* J. Lafaurie, "Le Trésor d'Escharen," *Revue Numismatique*, VIᵉ série, 1960, pp. 159–209.
** Dr. J. P. C. Kent of the British Museum Department of Coins and Medals, who has undertaken the study of the Sutton Hoo coins, also agrees with the earlier date.

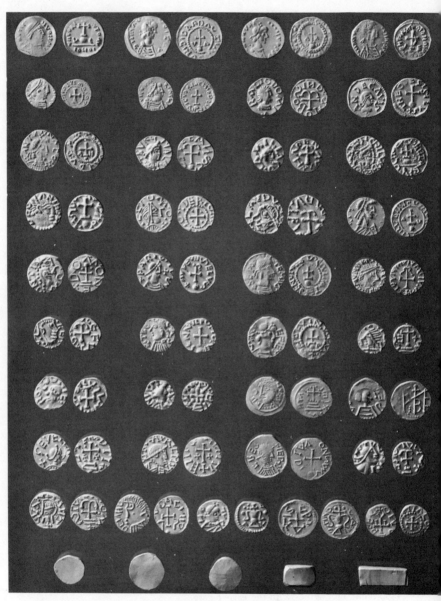

Obverses and reverses of the thirty-seven gold coins, with blanks and ingots, photographed from casts. Coins are grouped in pairs (1–37) from left to right. Pair number 1 is at the upper-left-hand corner. Numbers 26, 27, and 34 were probably struck in North Gaul. Numbers 7, 29, and 30 are unidentified. Three blanks and two ingots make up the bottom row.

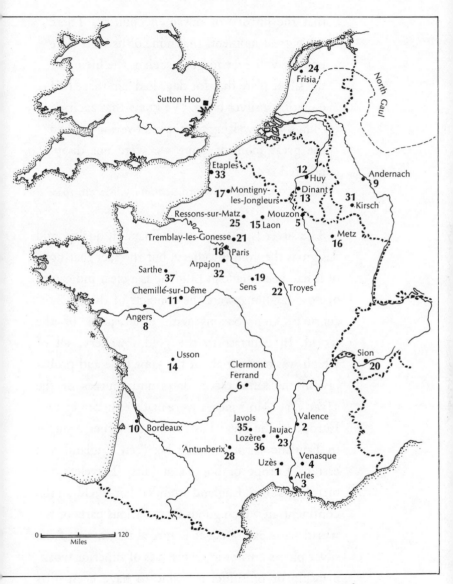

Map showing the locations of Merovingian mints at which coins were struck.

that the history of our own country. There were great moments that none of us who were present will ever forget—such as the lifting of the silver plate that for days had lain there half covering a silver basin. We knew that exciting things were waiting for the uncovering—when the great moment came we were not disappointed.

O. G. S. Crawford, *Antiquity*, March, 1940.

The silver is not so extraordinary in quality and design as the gold jewellery, but the fact that none of it had been made in England is a clear indication of how far-flung were the contacts of the seventh-century Anglo-Saxons with other parts of the world. In contrast to the gold jewellery, all of which was made at about the same time and probably in the same place, dates and sources of the silver vary. Most pieces were made either in eastern Europe or the Near East, and were either brought to England through trade between England and eastern Europe or bought at fairs. Travelers and merchants from England attended fairs, held on the continent, in which goods from various parts of the world were exhibited. It is agreed that most of the silver pieces are not in themselves of superior workmanship or of sufficient value to have been gifts from foreigners to English royalty. The nested silver bowls and the spoons are the only pieces that could have been conversion gifts.

THE SILVER BOWLS The silver bowls are about eight or nine inches in diameter, shallow, with an equal-armed cross inscribed on the inside. The design of the cross, somewhat different in each bowl, leads archaeologists to believe that the bowls have some Christian significance. They were made in a Byzantine province around the year 600. Only six of the original ten are on exhibit at the British Museum, since the others were either badly damaged or totally disintegrated. They have the soft glow and texture that is found only in old silver, with a depth and dimension that no photo can show.

THE SILVER SPOONS The two silver spoons, found under the mound of nested silver bowls, are of a classical style and are believed to have been made in some province of the Byzantine Empire. They are ten inches long; the handles, inlaid in niello, have the names Saul and Paul inscribed in Greek. Name inscriptions were not uncommon in early Christian and early Byzantine spoons, and frequently they

Two of the ten shallow silver bowls.

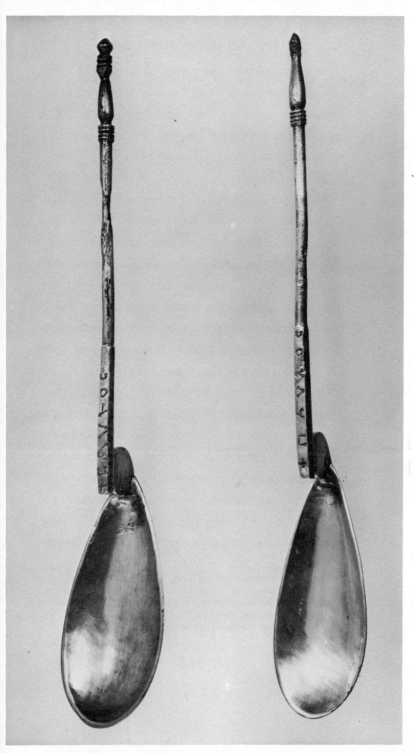

Pair of silver spoons, "Saul" engraved in Greek on the top spoon; "Paul" below.

were inscribed with the names of saints. The companion inscriptions clearly allude to conversion,* making the spoons a likely gift to a convert. The use of the spoons is not known: they may have had a liturgical use or they may have been merely sacred souvenirs.

An American scholar, Professor R. E. Kaske, who studied the spoons, does not think it likely that the name Saul would have been on a "liturgical" object. Professor Kaske believes that the engraving of Saul is actually an error and that the engraver meant it to be Paul. He noted how crudely "Saul" had been carved on the spoon, in comparison with the carefully done, symmetrical inscription of Paul. He thinks that the first letter, the ⌐ for P, has been incised ⌐, making it an S, because the engraver or copier started to put his letters vertically before he realized his mistake. Professor Kaske examined each letter in detail and describes how they show carelessness or inexperience. He thinks that the copier may have been working from memory, which accounts for the numerous errors. Professor Kaske has made an interesting and provocative ob-

* St. Paul, originally named Saul, a Jew who repudiated the teachings of Jesus, was struck blind on the road to Damascus, whereupon he had a vision that led him to accept the teachings of Jesus. He became Christian, changed his name to Paul, and became the most ardent of Jesus' disciples.

servation; whether his conjecture can be proved is another matter.*

Those who maintain that the burial was in honor of King Redwald point out that his conversion was of particular importance to the Pope, who was trying to advance Christianity in England and had had little success outside of Kent, Ethelbert's kingdom. East Anglia, farther north, was a growing power; Redwald was a rich and powerful king, and his acceptance of the new religion was politically important. Some think that King Redwald, after his conversion at the court of Ethelbert, might have carried his baptismal gifts—these very spoons and bowls—back to East Anglia with him.

THE ANASTASIUS DISH The Anastasius dish is an impressively large piece—28.5 inches in diameter. It is decorated with incised designs done in a pattern that appears too lacy and delicate for so large a dish. Experts do not consider it a piece of great beauty or of expert workmanship. They think that it was executed by an unskilled workman. Geometric crisscross patterns are combined with medallions and stars in an unrelated hodgepodge that appears to be the work of a craftsman who was fascinated

* R. E. Kaske, "Silver Spoons of Sutton Hoo," *Speculum*, October, 1967, p. 670-72.

by a variety of designs but who had no ability to select. Possibly the artist copied his patterns from a manual, and was influenced by the variety of details without giving much thought to coordinating the over-all design.*

The dish is of value to researchers because the four control stamps on the back have been identified as belonging to the Byzantine Emperor Anastasius I, and can therefore be dated to the time of his rule, 491–518. Since a study of the style of the dish points to its having been made around 400, researchers have suggested that the dish was made earlier and stamped one hundred years later.

The dish is in fairly good condition; only the edges are a bit corroded. The sides had been bent and the circular base badly crushed. It was straightened in the British Museum Laboratory.** Although the exact use of such a large dish can only be speculated upon, it would have made an impressive platter at a king's feast.

* Minutely detailed descriptions of designs on archaeological finds are of importance to students of antiquities, art history, and archaeology as an aid in studying and comparing similar designs on other pieces, and in identifying and dating finds. Those readers who are interested in more detailed descriptions will want to study the *Sutton Hoo Ship-Burial* by R. L. S. Bruce-Mitford.

** "It was toughened by heating it repeatedly with a large blowpipe flame and restored to shape with the fingers, and later with the help of a hide mallet." From H. J. Plenderleith, *The Conservation of Antiquities and Works of Art*, Oxford University Press, London, 1956.

2: *The Treasure*

Bowl with Classical Head Buried under the Anastasius dish was a fluted silver bowl, about 16 inches in diameter, with two drop handles. Its style is different from the Anastasius dish, and although it is also believed to be of Mediterranean origin, no parallel piece has ever been found. The bowl may have been made in Italy in the fifth century. The crudely executed female head in its center has been modeled along classical lines. The lady has bulging eyes and a double chin, and the scar on her cheek was left by the artist, who used a compass to define circular lines for inscribing an interior design.

Under the silver dish was found (in addition to the smaller silver bowl and other silver pieces) an iron axe-hammer, goose down,* cloth, leather bits of old shoes, a small ivory cylindrical object that may have been a piece from a board game, combs, two hanging bowls, and part of a leather bag. At the bottom of the lot was a rusted coat of chain mail that had been folded over so that the entire coat had rusted into an inseparable mass. All the finds under the Anastasius dish had been placed on a wooden tray. The excavators found evidence of rotted vegetable matter—an indication that the whole chamber had been strewn with bracken at the time of the burial. Mr. Phillips believes that the reason these

* Believed to have been part of a pillow. It was identified by an ornithologist at the Natural History Museum.

Fluted silver bowl with classical head; handles detached.

110

small and perishable finds were preserved was that
when the roof collapsed on the Byzantine dish they
were sealed between the dish and the wooden tray
beneath it.

The Ship

    Then they sailed, set their ship
Out on the waves, under the cliffs.
Ready for what came they wound through the
    currents,
The seas beating at the sand, and were borne
In the lap of their shining ship, lined
With gleaming armor, going safely
In that oak-hard boat to where their hearts took
    them.
The wind hurried them over the waves,
The ship foamed through the sea like a bird
Until, in the time they had known it would take,
Standing in the round-curled prow they could
    see
Sparkling hills, high and green,
Jutting up over the shore, and rejoicing
In those rock-steep cliffs they quietly ended
Their voyage.

BEOWULF: 210–224

III

The brilliance of the jewellery and the rarity of some of the other objects momentarily overshadowed the importance of the ship. Although the ship itself is lost, the complete outline of it remained. The rusted iron clench nails were in place in the soil exactly where they had once held the ship together. Instead of wooden planks there were stained impressions in the sand, and the excavators took extreme care that the imprint remain intact so that details of construction could be drawn. What kept every part in such perfect position was the heavy, wet sand holding every timber firmly in place as it slowly disintegrated, leaving only the nails.*

At first the ship was thought to be a Viking ship (9th–11th century), but examination of the impression revealed that it was from an earlier time and bore a similarity to the Nydam ship found in Schleswig in 1863. The Nydam ship, an ancestor of the Sutton Hoo ship, was in a good state of preservation, and was dated with certainty to the late fourth century. The Sutton Hoo ship was larger— 89 feet, whereas the Nydam ship was not quite 74 feet; the Sutton Hoo ship's greatest beam was 14 feet, and amidships the depth was 4 feet 6 inches; the Nydam ship's broadest beam was 10 feet, its

* See Chapter Five for an account of the process of taking a mold of the ship more than 25 years after the excavation.

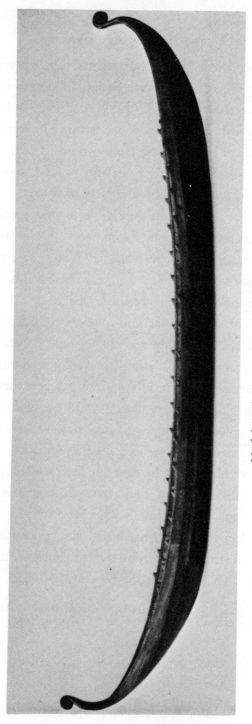

Model of the Sutton Hoo burial ship.

depth amidships 3 feet, 7 inches. The Sutton Hoo ship showed an advance in ship-building technique since the time when the Nydam ship was constructed. The strakes of the Sutton Hoo ship were made of several lengths, only an inch thick, riveted at overlapping joints. In the Nydam ship each strake was one continuous piece of wood.

The Sutton Hoo ship is the longest found that dates from the Anglo-Saxon period. Unfortunately, no trace of the prow remained. It must have risen at least twelve feet above the keel-plank amidship, and may have been elaborately carved.

The details of the ship were clearly traced in the ground.* The ship was clinker-built and had nine strakes to a side. Twenty-six were placed three feet apart except at the bow and stern, where they were closer. There were places for 38 oarsmen, and although no indication of a mast remained, some kind of sail might have been used. Neither the Sutton Hoo ship nor the Nydam ship had an effective keel, a deficiency that must have made maneuvering difficult. A large paddle was probably used to steer, and might have been located on a platform at the stern. Evidence of repairs in the hull revealed that the ship was old at the time of the burial. It may

* Details on the ship are in *Antiquaries Journal*, April, 1940, and in R. L. S. Bruce-Mitford, *The Sutton Hoo Ship-Burial*.

have been built some time in the latter part of the
sixth century, and probably it was in such boats
that the Germanic tribes came to England. Such a
sea voyage in an open ship must have been unpleas-
ant, with limited space for people, provisions, and
household possessions. The journey might have
taken months, and the passengers were probably
soaked as the waves constantly washed over the
sides. The sailors were dependent on the stars for
navigation and on manpower to move them
through the heavy seas. The work of rowing and
bailing must have been continuous. Doubtless the
journey was timed according to wind, tides, and
weather, and the immigrants would have kept close
to a shoreline so they could land if necessary.*

How did the Anglo-Saxons haul the heavy ship
up a 100-foot slope and overland half a mile to
lower it into the grave? Mr. Phillips believes that
the ship was moved forward on rollers and maneuvered so that it rested above the open trench on poles
or planks, along with cables that were held taut on
either side by bollards. The ship was lifted enough
to pull out the planks. Then, slowly, the cables
were played out, allowing the boat to settle into

* Charles Green in his book, *Sutton Hoo,* has discussed the
North Sea crossings at length, and has charted a hypothetical
voyage of two ships from Schleswig to England.

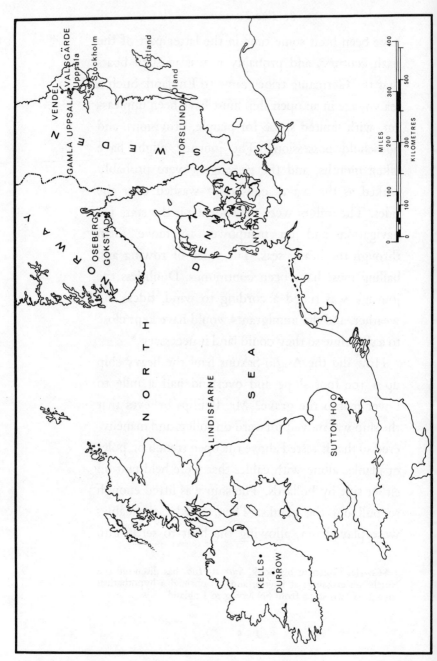

Map of northwest Europe, showing relation of Sutton Hoo to Scandinavia.

its firm-fitting trench.* The burial deposit was placed amidships, the cabin constructed and roofed over. The sand from the trench was shoveled in to fill the space between the ship and the sides of the trench, and some of the sand was placed inside the ship, firmly weighting it. Then the mound was built over the ship. What ceremonies and rituals accompanied this rite, how long it took, and what precautions had to be taken not to have the priceless treasure disturbed we may never know. "It is probably the finest monument of the pagan Anglo-Saxons that has come down to us, and the first known English war-vessel." **

* The BBC television film on the Sutton Hoo ship-burial illustrates this process with a small model.
** C. W. Phillips, "The Excavation of the Sutton Hoo Ship-Burial," *Antiquaries Journal*, April, 1940, p. 192.

CHAPTER THREE

THE QUESTIONS

And there they brought the belovèd body
Of their ring-giving lord, and laid him near
The mast. Next to that noble corpse
They heaped up treasures, jeweled helmets,
Hooked swords and coats of mail, armor
Carried from the ends of the earth; no ship
Had ever sailed so brightly fitted,
No king sent forth more deeply mourned.

BEOWULF: 34–41

Who Was Buried at Sutton Hoo? When Was the Burial?

THE SUTTON Hoo ship-burial was a cenotaph for one of the kings who reigned in East Anglia during the seventh century. But which one? The coins cannot be precisely dated, and the time within which the burial might have occurred ranges, according to present estimates, between 625 and 670. After that time Christianity was firmly enough established for a pagan burial on such a scale to be highly improbable. In nearly all early newspaper reports the Sutton Hoo burial was referred to as Redwald's grave, but after the initial study of the coins a burial date earlier than 640 was ruled out and Redwald, who died in about 625, was eliminated by most historians.

Most people are satisfied to know that the treasure was buried thirteen centuries ago. But to the historian, for whom facts are essential, verification of one fact is dependent upon another, and sloppy or vague conclusions multiplied would make his work valueless. While the answers to some of the questions that have arisen about Sutton Hoo must still be regarded as provisional until more evidence is in, a few points have been generally agreed upon: (1) The grave was a cenotaph because no evidence has been found of either inhumation or cremation. (2) The memorial was for a king, not a queen. (3) He was an English king, not a reigning conqueror or visiting royalty, and he was most likely one of the East Anglian kings.

No one but a king would have been buried on such an extravagant scale, and with the emblems of royalty—the whetstone and the iron standard. He was also buried with the gold fittings and strap-mounts, official regalia that could only have belonged to a king. No possessions were found that would have belonged to a woman, and since a woman would not have been buried with armor and weapons, it was not a queen. Few doubt that it was an English king because historical evidence shows that no foreign power ruled in England at that time. A foreign king who died while visiting would not have been accorded such an elaborate funeral. If it was an English king, most likely it was an East Anglian king, not a king from another part of England.

Assuming this reasoning is correct, important points to establish are, first, the date of the burial; second, which king's death coincides with that date; and, finally, whether he would have received a pagan burial. We know that after the establishment of Christianity the church insisted that Christian kings be buried in consecrated ground—either in a monastery or in a church.

No one knows who the first East Anglian king was. Bede records that the earliest kings were known as the *Wuffingas*, which suggests that the dynasty was founded by someone named Wuffa. The names of the East Anglian kings and the order of their reigns are known from a manuscript in the British Museum.*

The following lists only those East Anglian kings who died within the years when the burial might have occurred:

Redwald   d. 624 or 625

Sigebehrt
Ecric (Aethilric) | both killed shortly after 640

---

* Cotton Vespasian BVI, a document comprising genealogies and lists of bishops written in the early ninth century.

Anna   d. 654
Aethelhere   d. 655
Aethelwald   d. 663 or 664

Sigebehrt and Ecric (Ecric may also have been
called Aethilric) were joint rulers and it is not clear
what their relationship was. One writer * claims the
burial was for Ecric. Sigebehrt was in exile in
France until 630, and when he returned he might
have brought with him a purse of the latest gold
coins, either as gifts or as payments. In the early
640's the transition from the pagan to the Christian
age was taking place, and Ecric was at least nomi-
nally a Christian. Sigebehrt, who was converted
while in France, was a devout Christian. He eventually entered a monastery, leaving Ecric to rule
alone. But he was later taken from the monastery
by force, with Ecric's consent, so that he could help
to fight the Mercians, who lived in a north midland
kingdom on the border of Wales. Both Sigebehrt
and Ecric were killed soon after 640.

King Anna succeeded Ecric. Mrs. Glass pointed
out that a burial of such magnitude, using so much
of the royal treasury, could only have been carried
out *by* a king *for* a king. She reasoned that the

* Sandra Glass, "The Sutton Hoo Ship-Burial," September,
Antiquity, 1962.

Christian king Anna permitted the pagan warriors, who had survived the battle with Penda of Mercia, to erect a memorial for the heroic Ecric. Anna supplied not only wealth from the royal treasury but also the whetstone and standard, both heirlooms and royal *pagan* symbols which Anna may have wanted buried. After that, East Anglia became a Christian country.

Some claim that Anna did not do the burying but was the one buried. He is known to have been a devout Christian: he founded monasteries, and had several daughters who all became nuns. It is recorded that when he died in 654 he was given a Christian burial at Blythburgh; but some believe it possible that the pagan cenotaph at Sutton Hoo was also in his honor.*

Aethelhere, who succeeded Anna, died in 655 after a short reign. Although he was married to a Christian who eventually became a nun, he entered an alliance with Penda of Mercia, a pagan and an enemy of the East Angles, who had slain Aethel-

---

* "It is possible to imagine a thoroughly Christian king like Anna being commemorated in this way as a concession to public feeling when all were not yet Christians. A king who was personally thoroughly Christian would certainly be given Christian burial, but it might still be politically necessary, perhaps for the last time in this instance, to go through the motions of a pagan burial, and hence the cenotaph character of the ship burial." C. W. Phillips in a letter to the author.

here's brother Anna. Some have held that this was Aethelhere's cenotaph because his body was lost in flood waters during a battle at Winwaed, and this fits in with the absence of a body at Sutton Hoo. Others have argued that his reign was short and not particularly distinguished, making him an unlikely man to have been accorded such an elaborate funeral.

Aethelwald was a Christian king who acted as a godfather at a king's baptism and is known to have been responsible for the destruction of Redwald's strange altars to God and the devil. He died in 663 or 664, perhaps too far into the Christian era for him to have been accorded a cenotaph such as that at Sutton Hoo.

Until further study of the coins put their assemblage at an earlier date, scholars wrestled inconclusively with arguments in support of attributing the cenotaph to one of these kings. But the most recent studies * have dated the assemblage of the coins at about the year 625, and some now have returned to the speculation that the king honored at Sutton Hoo was Redwald.

Redwald, an early East Anglian king, attained the title of Bretwalda, or overlord of the kingdoms.

* J. Lafaurie, "Le Trésor d'Escharen."

3: The Questions

For that reason early speculations attributed the Sutton Hoo burial to him. He was the first East Anglian king to be converted to Christianity. But according to Bede, Redwald had "received Christian Baptism in Kent, but to no good purpose; for on his return home, his wife and certain perverse advisers persuaded him to apostasize from the true Faith. So his last state was worse than the first, for, like the ancient Samaritans, he tried to serve both Christ and the ancient gods, and he had in the same temple an altar for the holy Sacrifice of Christ side by side with an altar on which victims were offered to devils." *

The Christian symbols in the grave—the silver bowls decorated with the equal-armed cross and the two spoons on which the names Saul and Paul had been engraved—were found near what would have been the shoulder of the dead man if there had been a body. Doubtless the king commemorated at Sutton Hoo had at least some interest in Christianity. Bede records that on several occasions gifts were sent by the Pope to Saxon kings who were either commemorating or anticipating conversion.

The date of the assemblage of the coins agrees with the date of Redwald's death. It would have been fitting for him as Bretwalda to have been

* Bede, *A History of the English Church and People*, p. 128.

given an elaborate burial. Since he was converted at Aethelbert's court, he would likely have received gifts commemorating the event. With his unique altars to God and devil, he well might have been accorded a pagan burial. Possibly his wife arranged the ceremony. So far the pieces of the story fit together.

Where Is the Body?

Researchers are aware of no reason why Redwald's body could not have been placed in the grave. But they do know that it would be against any presently known pagan practice to find a cremated body amidst unburned grave goods. On the other hand, cremation was not compatible with Christian burial at that time.

Another question remains unanswered: How long after the assemblage of the coins did the burial take place? All that archaeologists are sure of is that the burial could not have taken place *before* 625.

What Was the Connection with Sweden at This Early Date?

Boat-burials dating from this early period have been found only in the Uppland province of Sweden and southeast Suffolk in England. Later, in the Viking period, almost two centuries after the Sutton Hoo burial, boat inhumation was widespread, and numerous boat-burials have been found in Norway and Denmark. The object of such a burial was to provide the dead with a means of transportation to the next world. He departed fully equipped for the journey, accompanied by necessities and luxuries for his next life—money, weapons, cooking utensils, personal possessions, family heirlooms, and so forth. The splendor of the burial and the size of the boat depended on the rank and wealth of the dead.

Many objects found in the Sutton Hoo ship were old at the time of the burial and cannot be precisely dated. The helmet, the shield, and the sword pommel have been identified as having been made in Sweden long before the date of the burial. Other objects, although of distinctly native workmanship, resemble in design those found in Swedish graves. Historians have concluded that these ancient possessions from Sweden were family heirlooms.

And the prince and his people will remember those
    treasures,
Will remember that their fathers once wore them,
    fell

With those helmets on their heads, those swords in
their hands.

BEOWULF: 2036–2038

If this is the burial of an English king carried out
according to Swedish custom, the grave containing
Swedish heirlooms, as well as regalia of English
make but of Swedish design, historians are tempted
to conclude that the East Anglian Royal House of
Wuffingas was of Swedish origin. Although historians assumed that migrations from Sweden took
place during the Viking period—that is, some 150
or more years after the date of the Sutton Hoo
burial—they now believe it likely that an offshoot
of the Royal House of Uppsala, named *Sculfings*,
migrated from Sweden some time in the middle of
the sixth century and founded the East Anglian
Dynasty.*

About four miles from Sutton Hoo is the parish
of Rendlesham, referred to by Bede as a royal residence, and possibly the place where Redwald, king
of the East Saxons, kept his court. About 1690 a
crown weighing 60 ounces was dug up in the area,
presumably made of either gold or silver because
it was subsequently melted down. Possibly Sutton
Hoo was the royal burial ground for Rendlesham.

* See Chapter Four, "Sutton Hoo and the Age of *Beowulf*."

The ship-burial was situated in such a way that travelers riding up the River Deben to the palace at Rendlesham could see the burial atop the 100-foot escarpment. The thick woods evident today were not planted until 1881, so the boat-barrow would have been visible from the river.

The Deben Valley could have been a gateway to trade and other influences from the south, thus making it a political center. It is hoped that with further excavations at Sutton Hoo, as well as further study of Rendlesham through aerial photography, some of these questions will be answered.

CHAPTER FOUR

SUTTON HOO AND THE AGE OF BEOWULF

ENGLISH *historians realized at once what Sutton Hoo suggested about Anglo-Saxon civilization at large, that its richness of culture and range of contacts with northern and southern Europe and the Mediterranean had been underestimated, and that the epic poem* Beowulf *was even less of a primitive fancy and more of a document of English social history than had been thought.*

J. B. Bessinger, "*Beowulf* and the Harp at Sutton Hoo," *University of Toronto Quarterly*, University of Toronto Press, January, 1958.

Bring me ancient silver, precious
Jewels, shining armor and gems.

BEOWULF: 2747–2748

Beowulf is the oldest epic in English, but scholars
have studied it for only about 150 years, a short
time compared with the number of years Classical
literature has been studied. Not all have agreed on
the literary merit of the poem. Opinions have
ranged from praising it as being "as sophisticated in
its construction and use of allusions as *The Waste
Land* of T. S. Eliot," * to calling it a "shapeless
monstrosity" with "barbarian merit." ** The final
judgment is not yet in. Few have disputed its value
as a storehouse of information on the Anglo-Saxon

* From David Wright's Introduction to his prose translation
of *Beowulf*, Penguin Books, New York, 1957, p. 13.
** Sir Arthur Quiller-Couch, *On the Art of Writing*, Put-
nam's Sons, New York, 1916, p. 196.

period, specifically: the aristocratic society, the relation of king and warrior, and the importance placed on loyalty and courage as primary virtues in man.

The story that the *Beowulf* poet wrote was an adventure tale about a heroic figure who undertook a dangerous mission to aid a foreign country. His battles with monsters and dragons are recounted in the somber tone of impending catastrophe. Now the Sutton Hoo finds have revealed that the poet has managed to weave some remarkably accurate descriptions into his story. The corroboration between poem and treasure is startling.

Many scholars believe that *Beowulf* was written some time in the early eighth century, possibly within seventy-five years, or less, of the Sutton Hoo burial. It is believed to have been the composition of one man describing life in the fifth and sixth centuries in a Scandinavian setting. It was written in a West Saxon dialect, the dialect of most of the surviving Anglo-Saxon manuscripts, but the poem might have had East Anglian origins. Paleographical evidence reveals that the only surviving manuscript of *Beowulf* was written in the tenth century by two different scribes: one wrote to line 1939 and the second completed that line and finished the entire poem, 3182 lines long.

The manuscript came to the library of Sir Robert

Cotton in the seventeenth century. Since it was placed on the first shelf beneath his bust of the Roman Emperor Vitellius and was the fifteenth book on the shelf, it has come to be known as Cotton Vitellius XV. After Sir Robert's death a fire destroyed much of his library and the *Beowulf* manuscript was badly damaged. Before it had deteriorated too far, a Danish scholar, Grímur Jonsson Thorkelin, became interested in it after seeing it listed in a catalogue issued by Humphrey Wanley in 1705. Wanley had incorrectly described the poem as the story of a Danish hero who had fought Swedish kings. Thus, through Wanley's careless error, Thorkelin's interest in the manuscript was aroused and he transcribed the poem in 1787. Eventually the manuscript was carefully treated against further disintegration and its fragile edges reinforced, but scholars are dependent upon Thorkelin's transcription for the passages or letters missing. Thorkelin's copy of *Beowulf* was destroyed by fire when the English bombarded Copenhagen in 1807. But another copy that he had had made was saved, and Thorkelin set to work to prepare an edition, with a parallel Latin translation, that was brought out in 1815.

In the opinion of the Swedish archaeologist Sune Lindqvist, the Sutton Hoo burial and *Beowulf* are

two documents that "complement one another admirably. Both become clearer by comparison." *
The Beowulf poem opens with the funeral of Shild
—or Scyld—a Danish mythological king. Like the
burial at Sutton Hoo, it was a ship-burial and the
treasure was laid inside the boat:

> There in the harbor was a ring-prowed fighting
> Ship, its timbers icy, waiting,
> And there they brought the belovèd body
> Of their ring-giving lord, and laid him near
> The mast. Next to that noble corpse
> They heaped up treasures, jeweled helmets,
> Hooked swords and coats of mail, armor
> Carried from the ends of the earth: no ship
> Had ever sailed so brightly fitted,
> No king sent forth more deeply mourned.
> Forced to set him adrift, floating
> As far as the tide might run, they refused
> To give him less from their hoards of gold
> Than those who'd shipped him away, an orphan
> And a beggar, to cross the waves alone.
> High up over his head they flew
> His shining banner, then sadly let
> The water pull at the ship, watched it

* "Sutton Hoo and *Beowulf*," *Antiquity*, September, 1948,
p. 140.

138

Slowly sliding to where neither rulers
Nor heroes nor anyone can say whose hands
Opened to take that motionless cargo.

                                    BEOWULF: 32–52

The difference between Shild's funeral and that at Sutton Hoo was that his ship, with its shining banner and hoards of gold, was set to sail rather than buried in the ground.

The entire poem glitters with such references as "silver shirts," "gold-carved shields," "gold-shining roof," "bright rings," "jeweled saddle," "gem-studded cup." Until the discovery at Sutton Hoo, no evidence supported the *Beowulf* poet's repeated references to the wealth of an Anglo-Saxon king, but now the archaeological evidence is in. "That loving connoisseurship of treasures of aesthetic appeal which is so characteristic in the artefacts of Sutton Hoo, is equally strongly felt in *Beowulf*, where there is the same suggestion of sheer joy in the contemplation and possession of treasures of the art of the goldsmith and the gem-cutter." * Now the references in *Beowulf* to glistening helmets can be better understood since the laboratory study of the helmet showed that the outer surface was

* C. L. Wrenn, "Sutton Hoo and *Beowulf*," reprinted in *An Anthology of Beowulf Criticism*, edited by Lewis E. Nicholson, University of Notre Dame Press, Notre Dame, 1963.

tinned and, when new, must have been very shiny.

Sune Lindqvist has raised other questions about the connection that the Anglo-Saxons might have had with Sweden. He writes: "If *Beowulf* really was written for a dynasty that prided itself on its northern origins, some member of that dynasty ought to be named in it." He ventures that the member was the brave and loyal Wiglaf, who joined Beowulf in his last battle with the dragon. The poet tells that Wiglaf came from a Swedish family. Some scholars believe that Wehha, mentioned in the royal East Anglian genealogy, may have been connected with Wihstan (or Weostan), father of Wiglaf. Professor Lindqvist raises another question: was the poet's purpose "to honour a Royal House—the Uffingas?—which proudly cherished its northern origins?" In Professor Lindqvist's opinion, it is not unlikely that *Beowulf* was composed "while many of those who had witnessed the burial at Sutton Hoo were still alive." *

Beowulf *and Treasure Trove*

The verdict regarding who was entitled to the Sutton Hoo treasure was directly influenced by

* "Sutton Hoo and *Beowulf*," *Antiquity*, September, 1948, pp. 131 and 139.

passages from *Beowulf*. British law defines Treasure Trove as something valuable—gold or silver—which had been buried or hidden for safety with the intention of recovering it in the future. Legally it belongs to the owner's heir, but if the heir is unknown, Treasure Trove becomes the property of the Crown. But the Crown must pay the finder its full value.

After the excavation at Sutton Hoo had been completed, a coroner's inquest was held on August 14, 1939, to determine whether or not the treasure at Sutton Hoo was Treasure Trove. Mr. C. W. Phillips pointed out that a prominent seventh-century leader would not have been buried in secret, nor could a mound, consisting of some 1000 tons of turf, have been made over the trench without it being publicly known. A passage was cited from *Beowulf*. At the end of the poem there is a description of Beowulf's funeral *:

The treasures they'd taken were left there, too,
Silver and jewels buried in the sandy
Ground, back in the earth, again
An forever hidden and useless to men.

BEOWULF: 3165–3168

---

* An additional point was made by Professor Wrenn in "Sutton Hoo and *Beowulf*." He pointed out that Beowulf was buried on a "hoh," meaning heel—hence promontory or headland. The "Hoo" of Sutton Hoo derives from "hoh."

The coroner's jury consisted of 14 members: retired military officers, farmers, a bank manager, a publican, a golf-club secretary, a haulage contractor, a village grocer, a land agent, a blacksmith, and a schoolteacher. They decided that the valuables had been buried with no intent to recover them, that they were *not* Treasure Trove, and, therefore, that they belonged to Mrs. E. M. Pretty, the landowner.

Few people have found a buried treasure right in the front yard, as it were. Having initiated the excavation, Mrs. Pretty financed it in its early stages, paid for police protection during the work, and, finally, gave it to the Nation. One wonders what would have happened to the Sutton Hoo treasure if Mrs. Pretty had not become fascinated by the curious mounds she viewed daily from her drawing-room window.

CHAPTER FIVE

SUTTON HOO NOW

The Sutton Hoo ship-burial constitutes by far the finest collection of evidence archaeologists have today on life in the Dark Ages of northern Europe.

R. L. S. Bruce-Mitford, *Scientific American*, April, 1951.

THIRTY YEARS have passed since the excavation of the Sutton Hoo treasure. The circumstances surrounding the dig were unique. With the immediate outbreak of war all the finds had to be hurriedly packed and placed somewhere for safekeeping, thus postponing detailed study and laboratory analysis. Those who worked on the dig at Sutton Hoo went immediately to various war posts. Nothing could have illustrated the dramatic timing of the close of the excavation more graphically than the issues of the *Illustrated London News* for the last weeks of August, 1939. Announcements and photos of the Sutton Hoo finds were given coverage along with reports on army training and general war news. A final notice about Sutton Hoo appeared in the issue of August 26. The following week, September 2, the cover photo of the *Illustrated London News* was captioned: "On Guard in Britain: A projector controller silhouetted against the beam of his searchlight, which reveals night raiders to defending fighter aircraft and A.A. guns." The stark black-and-white photo reminds one that the focus of every man was not on the mysteries of the past world, but on the preservation of the present one.

After the war those who had worked on the dig took up different positions: the immediacy and enthusiasm surrounding Sutton Hoo in 1939 had faded. It took Britain a long time to recover from the years of strain, deprivation, and destruction. Since Britain was preoccupied with getting back on her feet and adjusting to a changed world, only limited funds were left for studying and reconstructing the world of the seventh century. Now, at last, plans are being made to go ahead with the excavation.* The task of studying the finds is under the direction of Dr. R. L. S. Bruce-Mitford, Keeper of Medieval and Later Antiquities at the British Museum. He has a staff working solely on the Sutton Hoo finds.

During the Second World War the area of Sutton Hoo was used as an army training ground. The

---

* After the death of Mrs. E. M. Pretty in 1943, the property at Sutton Hoo was sold. Although it is still private property and, therefore, may not be visited without permission, the actual area of the mounds has been scheduled as an Ancient Monument. The British Museum has full rights to excavate, and ownership of any finds remains vested in the Pretty family.

ship-burial mound sustained some damage, but the excavation had been covered over sufficiently so that much of the outline of the impression remained. It was decided that further excavations beneath the impression might reveal important information, and this prompted the decision to take a plaster mold of the outline in an effort to preserve the remains of that massive and impressive document.

No such operation had ever been attempted in the history of British archaeology. Protected by a roof of nylon and polythene, the workers made the cast by dividing the enormous area into small rectangular sections. They used sand-filled polythene "sausages" to separate the blocks, and plasticene caps—more than 2000 of them—to cover the individual rivets. To keep the plaster from adhering to the sandy surface, it was found, after trying various materials, that paper toweling was most efficient. More than 6.5 tons of plaster were used, and the blocks, when they were set, were carefully marked and identified. Then these blocks were transported to the British Museum where fiber-glass impressions were made—fiber glass is lighter, and easier to handle and store than plaster. The casting operation took about three weeks, and excavations were carried on before and after.

During the work carried on from 1965 to 1967 the number of barrows was found to be 16, adding

Taking a plaster cast of the Sutton Hoo ship, 1967.

five more to the original 11. The soil that had been removed from the burial chamber in 1939 was carefully examined, a trowelful at a time, and several important finds have turned up: parts of the helmet and of the large hanging bowl, a boar's head, missing from the hanging bowl, and parts of the shield and standard. Beneath the ship they found split logs at the stern and bow that may have been used for manuevering the ship into position. Several hundred soil samples were taken to the British Museum Laboratory for careful chemical analysis in a further search for evidence of inhumation.*

The British Museum Laboratory is a comparatively new department. After the First World War a laboratory was set up to devise methods to remedy the ill effects of underground storage on some of the Museum's objects. As a result of that work, it was evident that there was a continuing need for a permanent research laboratory, and one was established as a separate department in the Museum. Extensive studies were made to determine effects of changing humidity and temperature, and the result was that after the Second World War no object had suffered. It was, according to Dr. H. J. Plenderleith, former Director of the British Mu-

* R. L. S. Bruce-Mitford, "Sutton Hoo Excavations, 1965–7," *Antiquity*, March, 1968. A description of the process of taking the mold, with photographs.

seum Laboratory, a triumph "for that particular branch of museum science cultivated in the fruitful no man's land lying between chemistry, physics, and biology on the one hand, and archaeology and fine arts on the other." *

The work of the science laboratory has expanded so that now conservation is only one aspect of it. There are new techniques of chemical analysis for the identification of archaeological finds as well as of art objects, and new methods of non-destructive testing by means of ultra-violet, X-ray, and microscopy. Problems that once existed, such as mildew, are now non-existent. Materials selected for mounting, binding, and repair work are carefully controlled; new kinds of paste and methods of applying it are constantly being tested; improved methods of treating corroded metals, leather, and textiles, have been found; faded writing can now be made visible by means of special photographic methods or by fluorescence.

At the British Museum one of the most important activities is reconstructing fragmented materials found by archaeologists. When evidence of totally disintegrated material such as bone or ivory is found, the scientist tries to determine what would have been the object's size and shape. Most important in conjunction with this work are the minutely

* *Illustrated London News*, November 18, 1950, pp. 827–29.

detailed written records kept by the field worker, and the careful photographic record. The International Institute for the Preservation of Historic and Artistic Work publishes a journal to circulate information on this new science to its members all over the world.

In a find such as that at Sutton Hoo, the laboratory scientist is aided by specialists from many fields besides archaeology and history, such as art history, linguistics, literature, numismatics, biological and physical chemistry, botany, ornithology, geology, navigation, and music.

The vast work at Sutton Hoo will be resumed after a delay of 31 years. An announcement in the London *Times* on August 21, 1967, reported that it was hoped that one mound a year might be opened over a period of twelve years, starting in 1970, under the direction of Dr. R. L. S. Bruce-Mitford. The story recorded here of the treasure at Sutton Hoo may be only the first in a series of chapters unfolding the mystery of the Anglo-Saxon period.

> the Almighty makes miracles
> When He pleases, wonder after wonder, and this
>   world
> Rests in His hands.

BEOWULF: 930–932

Selected Bibliography

The story of the treasure of Sutton Hoo has been woven from numerous articles that have appeared in professional journals, newspapers, periodicals, and books in the past thirty years. Two hundred or more items have been published and, obviously, not all can be listed here. The following lists some key publications on Sutton Hoo, and includes selected books on the Anglo-Saxon period.

Books on Sutton Hoo

BRUCE-MITFORD, R. L. S., *The Sutton Hoo Ship-Burial: A Handbook*. The British Museum, London, 1968. The most complete and up-to-date report of the finds at Sutton Hoo, with photographs. The notes provide a bibliography of all the scholarly work written on the subject. An indispensable guide for those who want to study the finds in detail.
Dr. Bruce-Mitford is writing a definitive four-volume work on Sutton Hoo, as well as editing his collected papers about the dig.
GREEN, CHARLES, *Sutton Hoo*, Merlin Press, London, 1963, reissued 1968. A detailed account of the dig with historical background and some interesting

speculations by Mr. Green. Excellent bibliography.
Photographs. For the advanced student.

Articles on Sutton Hoo

PHILLIPS, C. W., "The Excavation of the Sutton Hoo
Ship-Burial," *Antiquaries Journal*, April, 1940. The
first complete account of the Sutton Hoo excavation
by the man who conducted it.
———, "Ancestor of the British Navy," *The National
Geographic Magazine*, February, 1941.
———, "The Excavation of the Sutton Hoo Ship-
Burial," in R. L. S. Bruce-Mitford's *Recent Archaeological Excavations in Britain*, Routledge and Kegan
Paul, Ltd., London, 1956.
Antiquity, March, 1940, was devoted entirely to
articles on the Sutton Hoo ship-burial, written by
various people who were involved with the excavations or the study of the finds.
Speculum, January, 1954, contains a bibliography of
the Sutton Hoo ship-burial by F. P. Magoun. *Speculum*, October, 1958, includes a supplement to the
bibliography by J. B. Bessinger, Jr.

Selected Books on the Anglo-Saxon Period

BLAIR, PETER HUNTER, *An Introduction to Anglo-
Saxon England*, Cambridge University Press, Cam-
bridge, 1956. A short and readable history.
GROHSKOPF, BERNICE, *From Age to Age: Life and
Literature in Anglo-Saxon England*. Atheneum
Publishers, New York, 1968. An introduction to

the history, with selections from the literature, for readers with no background in the period. Photographs.

HODGKIN, R. H., *A History of the Anglo-Saxons*, 2 volumes, third edition, Oxford University Press, London, 1952. A readable and beautifully illustrated history that goes through the age of King Alfred. An Appendix on the Sutton Hoo ship-burial.

STENTON, F. M., *Anglo-Saxon England*, Oxford University Press, London, 1947. Volume 2 of the *Oxford History of England*. An authoritative history with an excellent bibliography.

WILSON, D. M., *The Anglo-Saxons*, Thames and Hudson, London, 1960. Volume 16 in *Ancient Peoples and Places* series. A readable account of the archaeology of the Anglo-Saxon period written by an archaeologist. Excellent photographs.

Selected Modern Translations of Beowulf

CROSSLEY-HOLLAND, KEVIN, *Beowulf*, Farrar, Straus, and Giroux, New York, 1968. In verse.

MORGAN, EDWIN, *Beowulf*, University of California Press, Berkeley, 1962. In verse.

RAFFEL, BURTON, *Beowulf*, New American Library, New York, 1963. In verse.

WRIGHT, DAVID, *Beowulf*, Penguin Books, Baltimore, 1957. Prose translation.

Professor J. B. Bessinger, Jr., has made a record in Old English, including parts of *Beowulf*, with some accompaniment by the Sutton Hoo harp. Caedmon TC1161.

Glossary

angons: iron throwing-spears.

aurochs: a wild ox, now extinct. Julius Caesar referred to the aurochs as an animal of great strength and speed, the hunting of which provided a trial of strength and courage for a young man of Germanic origin. The horns of an aurochs served as huge cups for drinking.

boss: a raised ornamentation, stud, or knob; a protuberant part.

Celtic: native British. The Celts were early inhabitants of Britain, who were pushed to the north and west of the island by the invading Germanic tribes.

charms: pagan chants, often accompanied by rituals that were supposed to ward off danger or disease. The oldest Anglo-Saxon poetry and prose are found in these charms.

clench nails: the end of a nail, or other fastening device, that is turned back on itself to hold fast or close tightly.

clinker-built: having the external boards or planks overlapping.

cloisonné: inlays of stone or glass in individual cells, built up on a base plate and arranged to form patterns. Cloisonné enamel, a Byzantine craft, did not appear in England until the ninth century.

control stamps: specific stamps on decorative pieces of Byzantine silver indicating that the piece met the standards of the Emperor, or Prefect of the city. Like a hallmark, the stamp was distinct and identifiable, and every piece of silver usually bore several control stamps.

Coptic: the Copts, descended from ancient Egyptians, belonged to the Christian Egyptian church that reached its high point in the sixth century.

die: a metal block or plate with an embossed design which can be used as a pattern.

escutcheon: a decorative device or emblem.

filigree: intricate, open-work design in fine gold, silver, or copper wire.

flambeau: a support for torches, often ornamental.

flan: a metal disk on which a coin design is stamped.

Franks Casket: a small box of carved ivory depicting scenes from legend, history, and the Bible. It was made in Northumbria about 700 and probably held jewellery or personal possessions. The casket was found in France in the nineteenth century and was presented to the British Museum by Sir Augustus Franks.

ingot: a mass of metal in any convenient shape for transporting or storing to be used later.

in situ: in the original position.

Merovingian: a dynasty of Frankish kings, reigning from A.D. 500–751, named after the first Frankish king, Meroveus. The Merovingian Franks occupied the area that is now France, Belgium, the Rhineland, and Switzerland.

millefiori: a bundle of glass rods of various colors is heated until the rods can be drawn out to a length of 30 or 40 feet. When cool the elongated rod is cut, and the cut sections showing the unusual cross-section pattern are inlaid on an enamel bed.

mount: a metal frame. A mount can enclose an ornament or an entire object.

niello: the process of incising designs on metal with a metallic alloy that leaves a deep black color. Before the tenth century, niello was a black paste made of silver sulfide.

shield-boss: see boss.

shield-mount: see mount.

strake: a single plank that extends from one end of a ship to the other. From Old English, *streccan,* to stretch.

sword knot: a tassel attached to the hilt of a sword.

terminal: forming the end of something.

tenon and mortise: a tenon is a projecting part cut on the end of a piece of wood or other material which can be inserted into a corresponding hole (mortise) in another piece to make a joint.

tigerware: stoneware that has a glaze which resembles the coat of a tiger.

Appendix

The Newly Reconstructed Musical Instrument

In 1948 the musical instrument (pp. 84–5) was reconstructed as a small, quadrangular harp, but additional fragments, originally thought to belong to the roof, proved to be part of the instrument.

Newly reconstructed in 1969, it is a round lyre, 29¼ inches long, 8¼ inches wide, with six gut strings each 20¼ inches long, of varied thickness and tension. It has been tuned to a pentatonic scale, with a pitch between alto and tenor registers. The new reconstruction is supported by comparisons with manuscript illustrations as well as with fragments of lyres found on the continent. Beaver hairs were identified on the outside of the frame of the instrument and it is believed that it was kept and buried in a beaverskin bag with the fur inward.

The maplewood fragments that led to the reappraisal had originally been boxed and catalogued as roof remains, and at that time it was thought that all that survived of the instrument had been contained in the bronze bowl. The old reconstruction was based on these fragments found in the bowl; many photographs were reproduced, and the music was recorded. But even if it was not an accurate reconstruction of the one in the Sutton Hoo burial, Dr. Bruce-Mitford maintains that it "is still of interest as recreating a type of instrument which it seems did exist in this era."

The relationship of the newly reconstructed instrument to the *hearpe* of *Beowulf* is discussed by Dr. Bruce-Mitford in a paper published in *Antiquity*, 1970. Dr. Bruce-Mitford was kind enough to supply the above information just as this book was going to press.

Index

Bernice Grohskopf

Bernice Grohskopf was born in Troy, New York, and grew up in Brooklyn. She graduated from Columbia University with a B.A. and M.A. in English Literature. Her previous books are *Seeds of Time: Selections from Shakespeare* (1963) and *From Age to Age: Life and Literature in Anglo-Saxon England* (1968). She lives in Upper Montclair, New Jersey, with her husband and thirteen-year-old daughter. Currently, Mrs. Grohskopf is working on another book about medieval England and also writing fiction.